Iris for Every Garden

Iris Ochroleuca

IRIS

FOR

Every Garden

SYDNEY B. MITCHELL

REVISED EDITION

Drawings by Tom Craig

M. BARROWS AND COMPANY, INC.

PUBLISHERS   •   NEW YORK

First Printing, October 1949
Second Printing, February 1950
Third Printing, November 1952
Revised Edition, June 1960

Contents

1128113

5

Illustrations

Foreword

Today, looking back over nearly a half century to the
time when as a student at McGill University in Montreal, Canada, I began growing and collecting irises (my work
in breeding new varieties dates from somewhat later), I feel
that I have lived through the great period in the development of the tall bearded iris, the finest hardy perennial for
our gardens. And now it seems that I am in at the beginning
of new adventures in the making of garden flowers from the
American beardless irises native to Louisiana and the very
different ones of the Pacific Coast. I am also seeing better
form and new colors in the tall spurias and in the Dutch
bulbous irises as well as improvements, both by importation
and American breeding, in the gorgeous Japanese varieties.
Most American gardens can now have a succession of irises
from May to August, and some in favored climates need not
be without some species or variety each month of the year.

My reason for writing this book is that with the exception
of the American Iris Society's manual *The Iris,* an invaluable
compilation, in the main made up of papers for the specialist
(I contributed one myself), there has been no new American
work on this subject for a couple of decades. I feel one is

needed which will appeal to the general gardener as well as the iris addict by its unity, comprehensive character, and emphasis on irises as garden flowers. This wide appeal I have endeavored to meet in this little book where the point of view has been that of the gardener, not the botanist, and where inclusion of material on minor species of little garden value has had to give place to adequate treatment of those irises most entitled to it for their beauty and ease of culture in our gardens.

This book has been planned and written for gardeners anywhere in the United States and Canada where irises can be grown and so is unlike my general garden books, which were frankly for readers in California and comparable climates. Not being a journalist but a gardener, I must have my roots somewhere and though they are now deep in the soil of the Pacific Coast they were transplanted from the Atlantic Coast, where for many years I had the largest amateur collection of irises on the continent. I have also lived in the Middle West and have some knowledge of the problems of iris growing there. Moreover I have been able to visit iris breeders and growers, amateur and commercial, in their gardens from Montreal to Los Angeles and from Seattle to Boston, as well as in England, France, and Italy, and have corresponded with fellow enthusiasts all over the world. It is from correspondence as Chairman of the American Iris Society Beardless and Species Committee that I have gathered information about the distribution of growers of other than the tall bearded irises, information still admittedly incomplete.

To achieve consistency, Bailey's *Hortus Second* has been followed for nomenclature even though I frequently prefer the usage of Dykes' *The Genus Iris*.

It is impossible here to thank every iris grower or writer

from whom some information has been obtained—we all stand on each other's shoulders. I do however owe a special debt to Tom Craig, Escondido artist, iris breeder, and grower, for the line drawings he has made for this book, and to Cooley's Gardens for permission to use exclusive color plates.

To my wife, who for weeks has had to submit to daily dictation from her husband—a temporary injury to my right hand prevented my writing the first draft—I am particularly indebted, especially for her patience with the temper of an author during the throes of giving birth to a book.

SYDNEY B. MITCHELL

May, 1949,
Berkeley, California.

FOREWORD TO REVISED EDITION

The publication of this new and revised edition of the late Sydney B. Mitchell's *Iris for Every Garden* fills the need, as the original did a decade ago, for a truly comprehensive work on iris for the general gardener as well as for the iris enthusiast. Prof. Mitchell was moved to write his book in 1949 because of the paucity of material on this subject. Because even now it is still the most significant work on iris written for the average American gardener, this new edition, revised and brought up to date by Molly Price (Mrs. John M.), an admirer of Prof. Mitchell and herself an eminent irisarian and writer on horticultural subjects, will be a standard reference for devotees of this flower and for beginners in need of palatable and digestible iris fare.

Mrs. Price has revised the book with Boswellian fidelity; she has faithfully maintained the point of view, even the style, of the author and has made changes and additions only where they have been necessitated by new developments in breeding, new varieties, new treatments for iris diseases, and advances in the various categories of dwarf irises, which are currently assuming greater importance in the modern gardening picture.

Prof. Mitchell was a librarian and educator by profession, a plantsman by avocation. He was well known and respected by iris fanciers the world over for his significant contributions to the development of irises. In association with the eminent breeder, William Mohr, he embarked on an intensive iris breeding program in the early 1920's. (Unfortunately, Mr. Mohr did not live to see most of the fruits of their joint labor—he met an untimely death in an automobile accident in 1923.) The work, however, was continued by Prof. Mitchell, who selected, named and introduced the iris seedlings that resulted from their combined efforts. Among these were such famous irises as Wm. Mohr, Santa Barbara, Frieda Mohr, El Capitan, Purissima, Los Angeles and San Francisco. San Francisco won the first Dykes Medal award to be given to an iris of American origin.

Some years later, Prof. Mitchell on his own strove for the creation of yellow irises of large size and clear color. His efforts were rewarded with great success, as every iris fancier will agree, with the magnificent varieties California Gold, Happy Days, Natanja and Fair Elaine. These later yellows and his white iris Purissima are in the blood lines of hundreds of the leading iris varieties of today.

Readers will find this book most informative, up to date and interesting, giving as it does, in clear and concise fashion, all the useful information needed to grow good irises in their gardens.

F. W. CASSEBEER

Iris for Every Garden

Bluebeard

Bazaar

Frances Kent

Violet Harmony

Mystic Melody

Blue Sapphire

Dwarf Red

Dutch Iris,
National Velvet

Japanese Iris, Gold Bound

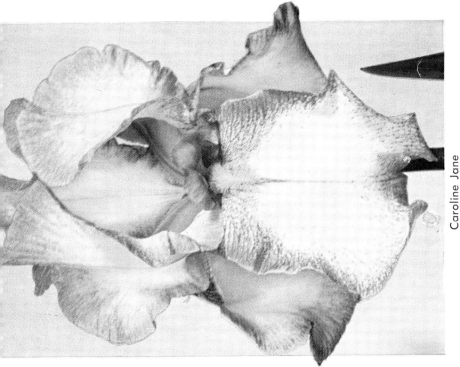

Caroline Jane

Limelight

Swirling Waves

Ivory Glow
Orchid Majesty

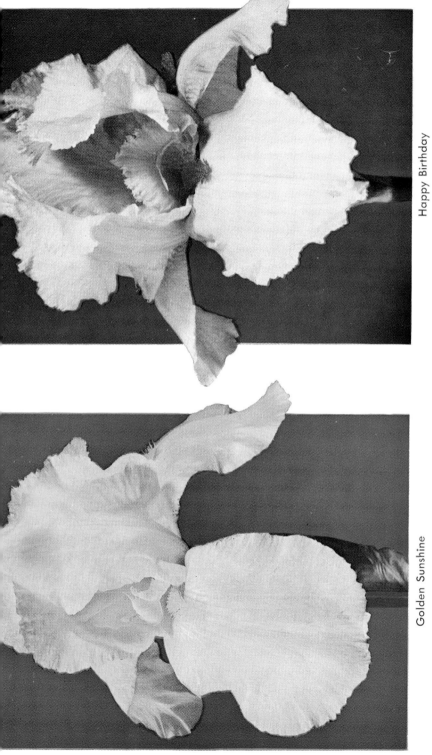

Happy Birthday

Golden Sunshine

Argus Pheasant

Lady Mohr

Irises for American Gardens

The idea of this book is to share with the reader a lifetime of experience in growing irises both on the Atlantic and the Pacific coasts, treating the subject in a way that will appeal to the general gardener as well as to the specialist. Emphasis is on those members of the iris family that lend themselves most easily to cultivation by the amateur, especially on the tall bearded irises. However, all species and their varieties which are amenable to garden cultivation have been covered. Besides lengthening the iris season, the species furnish plants for many different situations where the modern bearded hybrids are not always at their best.

Any classification of irises must be a botanical one, but as this book is written for gardeners by a gardener (not a botanist), technical terms will be kept to the minimum. A practical gardener's guide to the irises would enumerate four groups: the bulbous (with a basal bulb); the crested, the beardless, and the bearded (all three with rhizomes or fleshy rootstocks).

The bulbous irises store up food and go completely dormant in summer, so they can be lifted and stored. Examples are the dwarf early flowering members of the "reticulatas"—so-called because their bulbs have a netlike covering—and the junos, of which Iris bucharica is best known. More important for the average gardener are the hybrids which botanically belong to the xiphiums. Horticulturally they are referred to as Spanish and Dutch irises; here too belong the garden forms of Iris xiphioides popularly known as "English" irises.

Next come a few species known to gardeners as "crested" irises, which botanists group as the evansias. Here belong cristata, gracilipes, tectorum, and japonica with its relatives and hybrids. The rest of the family break into two great groups distinguished by the presence or absence of a fuzzy, hairy growth like a beard at the base of the lower petals or falls of the flowers.

The beardless irises, characterized by a fibrous root system and a fondness for water, comprise by far the largest number of species; several groups have been developed by breeding into garden races. All American wild irises are beardless. Among them are versicolor, fulva, foliosa, giganticærulea, and the variations known as Louisiana irises. Best known of the Pacific Coast natives are Douglasiana, tenax, and innominata. Of the Old World beardless irises the Siberians, the Japanese (forms of I. Kaempferi), and the tall, swordlike spurias are best known. Iris unguicularis and Pseudacorus are also in this group.

Most popular for gardens are the bearded irises with thick fleshy rhizomes and a preference for dry feet. For garden purposes the modern hybrid races are divided into dwarf, intermediate, and tall varieties. They all originally derived from species native to Asia Minor and southern Europe. These are now called Eupogons, that is, true bearded iris.

Related are two less common groups, the oncocyclus and regelia irises, the former with cushionlike and the latter with linear beards. Both are natives of Turkestan and Asia Minor and difficult to grow in most places. The best-known onco-cyclus is Iris suisiana. Of the regelias, Hoogiana is most grown, but more typical are Korolkowii and stolonifera, in weird oriental colorings.

CULTURE AND CLIMATE, PROS AND CONS

It is far more difficult to satisfy the needs of wildflowers in gardens than to grow the garden races. These are derived by selection of the tougher and more adaptable forms or by breeding new races with a far greater degree of adjustment to new conditions. Some wild irises, such as the natives of Louisiana and of the Pacific Coast, already possess a high degree of adaptability; the oncocyclus irises, on the other hand, are examples of rigid requirements.

The climatic conditions under which some irises grow naturally may be too different from those of your garden to justify much optimism in trying to raise them. Irises of the Siberian group from cold countries and marshy meadows will have little chance of being happy in a garden in Albuquer-que. Certain of the tall bearded iris species like I. mesopota-mica, with a tendency to make winter foliage, are equally difficult where there are long cold winters.

Soil and water conditions in the natural habitat of certain species also tend to limit their culture. Some grow in situa-tions where drainage is perfect, others where there are swamp conditions. While dogmatic statements regarding the prefer-ences of irises for alkaline or acid soils are unjustified, it is safe to say that many beardless irises including the Japanese have a decided preference for sour or limeless soils; the bearded irises, on the other hand, do well in a neutral soil and stand a good deal of lime.

All the adventure of gardening would be lost unless each of us were to try out in the garden a wide range of irises. Granted we can always depend on those which have already proved suited to the locality, still the peculiarities of an individual garden or the skill of the gardener in providing artificial conditions time and again achieve the apparently impossible. Years of writing about gardening have taught me the danger of saying that any plant cannot be grown under certain conditions. I have ceased to make such exact pronouncements, even though my forbearance deprive some readers of the simple pleasure of writing me gleefully that they have succeeded in doing the impossible. However, from my own experience, confirmed by that of others, I have ventured on the following observations on the possibilities of raising irises under varying climate conditions on our continent.

THE EAST

(Eastern Canada, New England, New York, New Jersey, Delaware, Maryland, District of Columbia, Pennsylvania, Ohio, Michigan, Indiana)

Dwarf bulbous irises, reticulata and bucharica, seem happy and permanent in certain gardens. Experience with Dutch and English varies from very successful at Amherst, Massachusetts, to a tendency in some gardens to get damaged and die out. Crested irises, except japonica, which is too tender, do well. Most beardless irises can readily be grown, the Siberians being very successful. However, unguicularis and the Pacific Coast natives need cold frame or other special protection for they do not endure open garden culture. All bearded irises except a few tender ones like Purissima thrive. Conditions are not favorable to oncocyclus, but regelia and regeliocyclus are reported doing very well under special culture.

THE SOUTH

(Tennessee, Kentucky, Virginia, the Carolinas, Georgia, Florida, Alabama, Mississippi, Louisiana, Eastern Texas, and Arkansas)

Bulbous irises do very well in the cooler southern states through Virginia and into North Carolina. The same region is also adapted to the crested irises except japonica, which is only hardy outdoors further south. Most beardless irises do well here and along the Piedmont: Japanese irises are features of gardens at Sumter, South Carolina, and in northern Mississippi. The southern natives are of course at home all along the coastal plain. In the drier, warmer hinterland trial should be made of unguicularis and the Pacific Coast natives. Bearded irises do well in much of this territory, though as one goes south culture changes somewhat. From Charleston on down to New Orleans and along the Gulf to eastern Texas, summers are too warm and moist for bearded or most other irises. Emphasis should be on the Louisiana species.

THE PRAIRIES

(Illinois, Wisconsin, Missouri, Kansas, Iowa, Nebraska, Minnesota, the Dakotas, and the bordering Canadian provinces)

This wide area is less hospitable to many kinds of irises than some others, at least in the northern half. Bulbous irises will need special protection and tend to be impermanent as one goes north. Of the crested irises, tectorum will do well in many gardens. Some beardless irises, the Siberians especially, will thrive; but only in the more southern states can great success be expected of the Japanese or the Louisiana irises. The bearded irises have been very satisfactory, particularly those bred by growers who introduced their cold-resistant varieties. Along the northern edge of the United States and across the Canadian border, even the bearded irises tend to winterkill. Perhaps only home breeding can produce a race which will be resistant to the often unfavorable conditions.

THE ROCKIES AND SOUTHWEST
(Arizona, New Mexico, western Texas, Oklahoma, Colorado, Utah, Nevada, Wyoming, Montana, Idaho)

Climate variations north to south make it unsafe to generalize. Conditions in Arizona bear some resemblance to those of California. Montana is more like the Prairie States. Growers of other than bearded irises have not been very numerous. Experiments such as have been undertaken by one woman in Oklahoma are necessary everywhere to show what more can be done with the bulbous, crested, and beardless species. The Siberians, spurias, and the native species missouriensis will succeed in most places, but the first are not rewarding in New Mexico because of summer drought. The bearded irises do pretty well throughout this area and are notably easy to grow in Denver and Colorado Springs, Salt Lake City, and other high places. Where there is altitude and dry summer heat the relatively difficult oncocyclus and regelias should succeed.

CALIFORNIA

Conditions here are fine for the small bulbous irises. The Dutch irises grow and flower well, but tend to develop mosaic. English irises can only be grown with special attention to cool location and watering. Iris japonica and its relatives thrive here as nowhere else. The beardless irises, unguicularis, the spurias, and the Louisiana irises are perfectly adapted to climatic conditions as are all Pacific Coast natives. The Japanese need special attention to soil and water. The Siberians are less happy and less floriferous than in colder climates, the related chrysographes and Forrestii quite difficult. Bearded irises, except those with much variegata or amoena in them, grow like weeds. Oncocyclus can be very successful at high altitudes but tend to be short lived near the Coast. Regelias and regeliocyclus are generally successful.

THE PACIFIC NORTHWEST
(Oregon, Washington, and British Columbia)

This coastal area is ideal for growing irises. Practically all bulbous irises, the crested species, and all beardless irises are very successful with certain tender exceptions like Purissima and the oncocyclus species, which need warmer, drier summers. Only in the coldest years are even unguicularis and japonica damaged.

CHAPTER TWO

An Iris World Tour

By following the trail of the irises from the Atlantic Coast westward round the world and making notes on their native haunts, much may be learned about the needs of different species in the way of favorable cultural conditions. Though many irises are adaptable, a knowledge of the soil and climate in which they have grown and survived in nature is of help to the gardener. Irises are found wild only in the Northern Hemisphere. South of the Equator they are replaced by the related moræas. So the trail leads straight across North America, Asia, and Europe, with only a little dip south to the African shores of the Mediterranean. Many irises grow only in very inaccessible places where visits to their homes would be impracticable for most of us. Fortunately, however, adventurous plant explorers have gone to most out-of-the-way places to collect seed or plants, and there is nothing to prevent our following the trail round the world in imagination.

THE ATLANTIC SEABOARD AND APPALACHIANS

Beginning our journey at the extreme Northeast of our own continent, the first species we should see is Iris setosa canadensis growing in Labrador, Newfoundland, round the lower St. Lawrence basin, and down along the coast of Maine.

Dr. Edgar Anderson reports it most accessible in great profusion along the highway below Rivière du Loup and on the Gaspé Peninsula. Here in flowering time, early summer, one can drive for hours through gray-blue iris fields. This iris is a remnant of the Iris setosa still found in northeastern Asia and in Alaska where it varies a great deal in size and height. At one time a broad belt of setosa undoubtedly girdled the northern part of our continent until the Ice Age obliterated all but the east and west fringes.

Much better known to most of us as the "common flag," Iris versicolor has spread far and wide from its original Appalachian home over the area from the Great Lakes through New York to New England and eastern Canada. Like setosa, it occurs in wetter places down the valley of the St. Lawrence. At home along creeks and streams or in marshes, the flag seems to favor open spaces, especially forest clearings.

On the southern fringes of versicolor's habitat we should find the violet or lavender Iris virginica. Practically indistinguishable to the average amateur, the two often grow side by side in marshy places and along sluggish streams. Iris virginica is the common iris from Ohio south to the Gulf of Mexico and in much of Arkansas and Texas.

Far different from these are certain little irises, all suitable for rock gardens, which we should find wild in the Appalachian Mountains. The choicest of these is certainly Iris cristata, the sole native of the small crested irises or evansias whose other members are all oriental. It grows along streams and on hills in Ohio, Kentucky, Tennessee, Virginia, Arkansas, and Texas, generally in cool moist soils in association with ferns, mosses, and violets. Its lovely little crested lavender flowers with orange ruffled hafts are carried on three- or

four-inch perianth tubes. Very closely allied to cristata is
Iris lacustris, the lake form, which is smaller and darker and
not so easy to grow. This we might see around Lakes Superior and Huron, particularly along the east shore of the
latter.

In the southern Appalachians we may expect to run across
a unique little dwarf, Iris verna, not unlike a small pumila
iris. Lilac-blue with a central orange band suggestive of an
adolescent beard, verna is nevertheless classed as an "apogon"
or beardless species. Not too common anywhere, but fond of
cool acid soils, it makes a choice rock garden subject. In
somewhat the same area and in the Blue Ridge and the
Piedmont, we should see prismatica, the only American iris
classified among the sibiricas. It has violet flowers on eighteen-inch stems, though dwarfer forms are also found.

LOUISIANA, MISSISSIPPI VALLEY, ROCKY MOUNTAINS

From Ohio towards the delta of the Mississippi we should
find over wide areas three species which are characteristically
swamp plants. Iris foliosa, so-called because of the abundant
foliage among which its blue flowers nestle, ranges from Ohio
through Kentucky, Missouri, and Arkansas to Texas, and in
the lower Mississippi Valley. Iris giganticærulea, which has
somewhat the same distribution, resembles foliosa, but grows
much taller, its usually blue flowers held well above the
leaves, with many varying forms. Perhaps the most exciting
of these southerners is the third: Iris fulva makes up for the
relatively small flower of the typical form by its coppery red
or terra-cotta shades. Though similar in distribution, it is
more concentrated around New Orleans. All three species

flower in April. Until a couple of decades ago, they attracted little attention from anyone but a few Louisiana gardeners who began to dig up especially attractive forms for their gardens.

In 1927 Dr. John K. Small of the New York Botanical Garden visited Louisiana and found in the environs of New Orleans so many different pleasing irises that he gave them much publicity, claiming specific rank for many. According to later verdicts however, they are for the most part variants or hybrids of foliosa, giganticærulea, and fulva, which in certain parts of Louisiana grow together. To their credit, Louisiana gardeners and lovers of the native flora have since explored other areas of the state, finding many lovely large flowers which they have domesticated in their gardens.

The center of the many attractive variants seems to be Abbeville, about 250 miles west of New Orleans. This is the Cajan country, the land occupied by the Acadian French whose expulsion from their Canadian homes is chronicled in *Evangeline*. Over this low flat coastal region flowed the Mississippi River in earlier ages, and, according to one theory, brought down seeds of these irises from higher, colder climates. This would explain their hardihood in gardens much farther north. Blues, purples, pinks, roses, whites, and wonderful pure reds—possibly new species, probably natural hybrids—grow wild in marshy places, cypress swamps, and along the bayous where their blossoms are often reflected in black water, and where you must take care along the trail not to step on deadly moccasins sleeping in the sun.

As we travel westward to the Rockies in search of irises, we shall see nothing new, only Iris missouriensis which is not exciting. Different forms of this iris will crop up all the way from New Mexico and Arizona through Colorado, Montana, and Idaho, to eastern Washington. Though more common east of the Sierras and the Cascades, missouriensis appears in a few highly restricted areas in southern California, notably on the shore of Big Bear Lake in the San Bernardino Mountains, and in Tulare County in the San Joaquin Valley. Usually growing in mountain meadows where there is water near the surface in early summer, or in marshy fields, it is quite attractive in masses as its lavender flowers are carried on stems about two feet in height, well above the deciduous foliage.

PACIFIC COAST SPECIES

Outside of Louisiana, we shall discover the greatest variety of natives along the Pacific Coast, especially from Monterey Bay in California northward into Washington. Though certainly less spectacular than the southern species, the Pacific Coast irises have a charm of their own.

Because of its close relationship to Iris missouriensis we should first note what seems to be the exclusively California longipetala. Though very much like the Rocky Mountain species, longipetala has evergreen foliage, generally larger flowers, and stems less noticeably above the foliage. Concentration is in central California, mostly around San Francisco Bay. Until highways and industrial sites eliminated the winter swamps in South San Francisco, it was very abundant there. As these swamps dried out in summer, Iris longipetala evidently needs no summer water.

In the San Bernardino Mountains of southern California we might find scattered colonies, not fields, of a lavender and purple iris usually classed as Iris Hartwegii. This differs in

appearance from the same species as found in the Yosemite
Valley and the northern Sierra Nevada, where it is generally
a pale creamy yellow with deeper veins, not a particularly
attractive member of the family. Both forms occur in the
pine woods where there is real winter weather. In the south
the flowers do not appear until June, after which the plants
die down under the fierce summer heat.

From Monterey north along the coast and in the near-by
mountains, Iris Douglasiana would be most evident.
Through open woods and along the mesas near the ocean,
patches and even great fields may be seen as far north as
southern Oregon, flowering in April in the south and in May
farther north. Iris Douglasiana can be identified by its abundant, broad, evergreen foliage, red at the base, and by its
fairly tall, branched flower stems, usually from a foot to two
feet high. The size and color of the flowers differ widely in
local areas. White, cream, pink, and blue-purple give some
idea of the color range of this species, which is easily adapted
to gardens where winter cold is not too severe.

Iris macrosiphon, though lovely, is far less common. Its
blue- or red-purple flowers on stems about three inches high
are overtopped and somewhat concealed by narrow slender
foliage four times that height. This species grows on Mount
Tamalpais near San Francisco, and there is a nice colony of
it north of the roadside just as you begin the climb from
Hopland to Lake County.

In western Oregon and Washington we should find Iris
tenax growing wild on hillsides and in meadows. A daintier
plant than Douglasiana, it has slenderer pale green foliage
and much shorter, perhaps six- to ten-inch unbranched flower
stems, with a similar wide range of flower colors—orchid,

lavender, purple, white—many with a paler zone on the falls. Iris Gormanii, with flowers of soft yellow or apricot, is now rated just a form of I. tenax, and a very attractive one.

Other Oregon natives worthy of our notice are Iris bracteata and Irish innominata. Named for the bractlike leaves which clothe the stem, the former is fairly common and its pleasing yellow flowers, veined brownish purple, are quite distinctive on stems about eight inches high. This is a plant of scant foliage and reputedly hard to move. Iris innominata we should find in the wild only if we took to mountain roads in very rough country. Dr. Matthew C. Riddle, of Portland, who has explored its haunts for years, locates innominata in southwestern Oregon in the territory of the lower Rogue River, the Illinois, and two small coastal rivers, the Elk and the Sixes, where winters are relatively cold and wet, summers hot and dry. So remote that it was not identified for just about a hundred years after other Oregon irises were named, it is easily first choice of our natives for the rock garden. Its foliage is grasslike, dark, and permanent; and it makes nice compact clumps from which the typically orange flowers appear above the leaves, some only two or three inches, some higher. The colors vary in the depth of yellow and of veinings, and there are blues and variegateds.

Gardeners of the Pacific Coast have strangely neglected their lovely native irises, the culture of which will be treated in Chapter Five. Now they are following the example of Louisiana gardeners and collecting, raising from seed, hybridizing, and improving specimens so close at hand and so perfectly adapted to their conditions.

The next leg of our round-the-world iris tour takes us far north to Alaska where we shall meet again Iris setosa, with which we began our journey. Here and there in adjacent Asia, setosa varies far more than on the Atlantic Coast, including some attractive forms for garden use—if you can get them.

I have treated our American native irises at some length because we can enjoy them wild even before we domesticate them. Following the trail across Asia and Europe, we shall have to be content with glimpses here and there.

IRISES OF THE ORIENT

Over on the Asiatic mainland we would naturally expect to find Iris sibirica. This, however, was wrongly named an Asiatic species, and we shall not see it until we reach Europe. However, in Manchuria and Japan we should discover a very close relative called Iris orientalis. Most gardeners and even some botanists consider this just a variety of sibirica, but the wide foliage, much shorter flower stems, far larger deep purple-blue flowers, and noticeably reddish bud spathes readily identify orientalis.

Another native of Siberia, Manchuria, Korea, and possibly of Japan is the water-loving Iris laevigata, the finest perhaps of all the blue beardless irises. It is often confused with Iris Kaempferi which is native to much the same area and is the species which was used by the Japanese in getting the garden plants we know by the name of Japanese irises.

In Japan and nowhere else do we find growing wild the crested Iris gracilipes, a dainty slender pinkish lilac flower on a ten-inch stem, fond of cool, damp, woodsy places. Another crested iris at home in Japan and also found in central China is japonica. With its evergreen foliage, much branched stems of eighteen inches or more, and many short-lived lavender flowers with deep yellow centers, japonica is one of the few irises that tolerate shade—in fact, prefer it. Among japonica's relatives are Iris Watti of southwestern China and Iris tectorum which is popular in Japan though native to central and southwestern China.

In the almost inaccessible mountains of western China, plant explorers like E. H. Wilson, George Forrest, and Kingdon Ward have in our own century found and made available for gardeners a number of irises, most of them members of the sibiricas. In 1895, Abbé Delavaye discovered in the swamps of Sze-Chuen the iris that now bears his name, much like a taller, larger, later Siberian with blue- or red-purple flowers. Iris chrysographes was found wild in southwestern China. Its deep rich red-violet flowers with varying veining of gold radiating from the base of the falls make it a lovely species for a wet place. A somewhat similar species in pale yellow, Iris Wilsonii, is native to western Hupeh and Shensi. More pleasing in the garden is Forrestii, a native of high alpine pastures of China, with delicate clear yellow flowers.

In Kashmir in northwestern India, we should meet Iris aurea, a tall three- to four-foot plant with swordlike leaves and stiff stems so closely branched that the golden yellow flowers seem to rise from them in vertical series. This is one of the spurias, of which there are numerous members in Asia Minor and Europe. In Kashmir, too, we discover our first tall bearded iris, kashmeriana, which may figure in the parentage of such fine whites as Purissima and its children. This, however, is a controversial point.

Turkestan is the home of the regelias, of which Korolkowii, stolonifera, and Hoogiana are best known. Strange and beautiful flowers from a country of bitterly cold winters and hot dry summers, the regelias are easier to grow in our gardens than their oncocyclus relatives from farther west. Here, too, we encounter the first of the peculiar group of bulbous irises called junos. Of these, Iris bucharica, from near-by Bokhara, is best known in American gardens. It is easily distinguished by the yellow and white flowers appearing in the axils of foliage like miniature corn.

From Persia north and west to the Mediterranean can be found the weird and sometimes beautiful oncocyclus irises, of which I. susiana is the only species much grown in America. Many oncocyclus species are natives of Palestine. Their natural conditions of winter cold and covering snow, fiercely hot and rainless summers are hard for us to match. Iris Gatesii and I. iberica are only names to American gardeners today, but they were once available and appear in the parentage of such distinctive modern irises as Lady Mohr.

In Asia Minor, the fine spuria, ochroleuca, favors places which are wet in winter and dry in summer. More important for us to note is the series of tall bearded irises of this region —mesopotamica, cypriana, trojana, and amas. Although we may think them gawky and awkward in growth, this series provided the large lavender or purple flowers on tall branched stems, which are characteristic of our modern hybrid bearded irises.

EUROPEAN IRISES

Across Europe from Greece to Spain, all along the Mediterranean, we shall meet with a great variety of irises. Either as found in nature or now in improved garden forms, these European species have furnished American gardens with much interest and beauty. From Austria, Hungary and the

Caucasus comes Iris pumila and from southern France and northern Italy comes Iris Chamaeiris, parents of many of our dwarf or short-stemmed bearded irises of early season. In Hungary we find variegata, with yellow standards and red falls; and in the Balkans and Italy we shall recognize forms of pallida, mainly lavenders and blues. The combining of these species gave most of the bearded garden irises bred up to half a century ago, though now superseded in all but old cottage gardens.

In central and southern Europe we should be greeted by many smaller blue spurias. The tall hollow-stemmed sibirica is from this same area, far from Siberia, and grows in marshy or at least moist places. Greece, the Aegean Islands, and Algeria are the homeland of Iris unguicularis or stylosa, so useful to gardeners in California for its winter flowers.

In Sicily, North Africa, and Spain we pick up the trail of the bulbous irises. Iris alata is a lovely early blue of the juno type. Here and in Portugal grow the wild parents of the Spanish, Dutch, and so-called English irises of our gardens. The xiphiums from the South favor dry conditions, the xiphioides from the Pyrenees, prefer to grow where it is wet. Both have given us good garden plants.

Almost anywhere in Europe we are sure to find the tall yellow Pseudacorus in flower in June, generally in low land wet in early summer. This is the closest relative of our own American versicolor growing near where we began our iris tour around the world.

CHAPTER THREE

Irises from Bulbs

1128113

R elatively few general gardeners or even iris specialists
have grown those members of the iris family which
have true bulbs rather than rhizomes or fibrous root systems
of permanent character. This neglect may be due to lack of
knowledge of their variety, interest and beauty, for the bulbous irises not only provide us with dwarf early subjects for
the rock garden but in the case of English, Spanish, and
Dutch varieties give us the specimens best suited to cutting,
far better than the widely grown bearded irises. It is true
that most bulbous irises have rather specific requirements
which cannot be met in every American garden. Yet all those
discussed here have been grown successfully by many gardeners who have reported good results from New England to
California and from Quebec to British Columbia. The central continental area is less hospitable to their cultivation
than the broad strips closer to both Atlantic and Pacific
Oceans.

One factor in the limited distribution of bulbous irises in
gardens has been that during the last decade the bulbs have
not been widely offered commercially, a situation which
shows signs of improvement. When you find them listed in
American catalogues, their cost even there is low compared
with that of most bearded irises; this is particularly true of

novelties. If you choose to import them from Dutch or English dealers, most bulbous irises are so inexpensive that almost any gardener can afford to make a trial of them and replace them in case of loss.

THE JUNOS

One group of bulbous species with certain characteristics in common has been named the juno irises. They have bulbs with several fleshy, thonglike, persistent feeding roots which are apt to become detached or broken in the process of digging and shipping: this is a decided drawback because the roots seem to be quite necessary to the flowering of these species. Their foliage consists of deeply channeled leaves set alternately on the stem, the flowers developing on short stems from the bases the leaves. The foliage is distinctive and suggests miniature Indian corn. The junos, as we discovered on our iris world tour, are found wild in Turkestan, Asia Minor, and around the western Mediterranean.

Iris alata is native to southern Spain, the North African coast, and Sicily, where it is found on the slopes of Mount Etna. In southern Spain it grows high up in the mountains as well as down in the valleys only a few hundred feet above sea level. I first saw it in January on the road from Cordova to Seville, great drifts of lavender-blue, the clumps of bulbs thriving in the gravelly well-drained soil. The dwarf foliage was almost hidden by the masses of lovely vanilla-scented flowers of which a single bulb will usually produce two or three in succession. We naturally coveted it for our California garden where climatic conditions rather resemble those of southern Spain, though our summers are less hot.

Through an English dealer I imported bulbs with the feeding roots intact; for though W. R. Dykes, the iris authority, says that even without these, alatas may flower the first year, they are usually too weak to do well afterwards. The imported bulbs flowered quite well the first year shortly after Christmas, but the amount of bloom diminished each year thereafter and they ultimately disappeared. E. O. Orpet, a great gardener who specializes in unusual bulbs in his Santa Barbara nursery, procured seed from Spain in 1931 and raised a lot of Iris alata from it; a dozen years later only one plant remained. He wrote me that for a time this iris was grown at Chico in the Sacramento Valley but did not multiply.

My own experience was that alata flowered in five years from the sowing of seed; since then it has been slowly dying out, though my last bulb flowered again this spring. Perhaps this iris needs better drainage and more summer baking than it gets here on the cool California coast. It is to be hoped that adventurous gardeners in the interior of southern California and in Arizona will attempt to grow alata when bulbs may be obtained. Its nearest relative botanically, Iris persica, with blue-purple flowers, blooms a month or two later and is apparently easier to raise and more permanent. However, I cannot find record of its being grown at present in America.

Iris bucharica is adapted to garden culture under conditions widely different from those of its native Bokhara. Success in flowering and in keeping it has been reported from New York, Michigan, California, Oregon, and the provinces of Ontario and British Columbia. This taller juno has stems a foot or more in height with as many as seven white, yellow-bladed flowers in the axils of the stem in early spring. Bucharica likes good drainage but makes no great demands as to soil. It can either be lifted in summer, when the foliage has ripened, and replanted in autumn or, if it is happy, can be left for years undisturbed and undivided, as my bulbs are casually treated here in California.

Iris bucharica
12"

Iris orchioides, with flowers of deep golden yellow, resembles bucharica and is not difficult. For some years I grew sindjarensis, which was somewhat more delicate than bucharica. This flowered for several years, though under our careless culture it later left us. Recently these and two newer species, vicaria, a robust growing juno with white, blue-tinged flowers, and Graeberiana, with cobalt-blue flowers, have been listed by a noted Dutch bulb firm. Warlsind is offered by a California grower. Success with them is reported from near Buffalo and, of course, in the Pacific Northwest. The correspondent near Buffalo writes that if you give the junos a good stiff soil and leave them alone they all perform quite nicely, and that he believes anyone who can grow lilies should be able to grow junos as the handling is very similar. (This report does not cover alata, which he does not grow.)

THE RETICULATAS

Very different little bulbous irises belong to the group of which I. reticulata is the type. A native of the Caucasus it is widely grown in American gardens and has proved easy and permanent in the Atlantic Coast states, Ontario, Quebec, Michigan, and all along the Pacific Coast from California to British Columbia. The small bulbs are best planted in autumn in well-drained soil, in a rock garden or along a path accessible in early spring when they flower. The effect is much better when the bulbs are so grouped that the lovely little sweet-scented blue-purple flowers with golden centers, appearing among the overtopping foliage, will not seem sparse or thin. They have done well where the bulbs were left in the ground and also where they were lifted, cleaned, and replanted in late summer or early autumn. Unfortunately they are sometimes attacked by a fungus which blackens the skin. Soaking in a solution of one part of formalin to three hundred of water is recommended for those only slightly affected, but as the bulbs are inexpensive most gardeners discard diseased stock and start a new planting in another place.

There are now to be had in Europe and, happily, recently in America several forms of Iris reticulata, some of them apparently crosses with the related Iris histrioides: such are the reddish purple J. S. Dijt, the Cantab (pale blue), Hercules (bronzy violet), Royal Blue, and Wentworth (a rich purple). Also in this group is the charming little yellow Danfordiæ. Iris histrioides flowers early and except in the milder parts of the Pacific Coast its blue-purple flowers are likely to be damaged unless grown under glass. In my experience the rarer January-flowering Histrio is not likely to be permanent unless the conditions are very favorable. Where spring is too cold and rough to have these little irises outdoors they may be grown in pots, several bulbs each, and under cool culture will flower well.

ENGLISH IRISES

Under the name of "English" irises, a bulbous species, Iris xiphioides, found wild only in the Pyrenees, has been widely distributed in its many garden forms by Dutch bulb growers. As the Dutch originally imported their bulbs from Bristol, they wrongly assumed that this iris was a native of England, hence its misnomer. In the wild its beautiful broad-petaled flowers are typically dark blue, but through generations of seedlings, color variations have come in without crossing with any other species. Where they can be grown successfully these irises are beautiful in the garden and handsome as cut flowers, but they have some natural limitations as well as others due to the poor condition in which the bulbs are often delivered from Europe. Their home in the alpine meadows of the Pyrenees is snow-covered in winter and wet through spring and summer; water is never far below the surface of the ground. Consequently xiphioides needs cool moist conditions through its period of growth, which lasts until August. It is never happy in hot dry soils or where summers are rainless.

It thrives best in the Pacific Northwest and can be grown with great ease in the Puget Sound country and in coastal British Columbia. It can also be grown on the Atlantic side of the continent. In a bulletin from the Massachusetts Agricultural Experiment Station, "The Bulbous Iris and Its Cultivation in Massachusetts," 1936, are given the results of a ten-year experiment at Amherst. In spite of the rather rigorous climate a large number of varieties were successful, though no special conditions were provided. Most of the bulbs originally planted at Amherst were grown in the Pacific Northwest; very few were imported from Europe.

Amateurs in New York State, eastern Canada, Ohio, some of the Rocky Mountain states, and in California have reported some success with English irises, though never comparable to what is easily achieved on the North Pacific Coast; in a good many cases after a year or two of flowering the plantings petered out. Where the desired culture can be given and they are still not successful, the difficulty probably lies in the condition of the bulbs when imported: they are rather soft and easily damaged in rough packing or long voyages. It is better to start with stock from Oregon, Washington, or British Columbia even if bulbs grown there are necessarily more costly than imports. Get bulbs, if possible, in August or early September and plant them at once in deep rich soil which is naturally cool and moist or can be kept so by watering. The preference is for neutral or acid rather than alkaline soil; where necessary add peat, leaf mold, or rotted pine needles.

Do not attempt to clean up xiphioides bulbs or remove off-sets, but plant them as received, about five or six inches deep. In very cold areas some protection by means of pine boughs may be desirable, but in most places where they can be grown they will not suffer from the cold; for though root growth begins early in fall the tops do not appear until early spring. Plantings should be watered not only until they flower in June or July but into August when the foliage begins to turn yellow. Lifting and replanting is best done in late August, the bulbs left out of the ground for as little time as possible, as they do not store well. In replanting, divisions or offsets should only be removed if they break away readily. Where bulbs are doing well they need not be lifted for three or four years.

My own first attempt to grow xiphioides in Berkeley was with bulbs imported from Holland. It was a complete failure. I got no bloom even the first spring and the bulbs soon disappeared. Last year I selected a half-shady place and planted in autumn some good sound bulbs sent me from British Columbia. They flowered fairly well in May and June. I continued to water them all summer and note this spring that they are pushing up strong growth, so apparently they are going to stay with me for a while.

Though there is no evidence that the Dutch growers have been active in recent years in raising new English irises, this has not been necessary. A series of good named ones, already accumulated, pretty well covers the range of color from white through pale blue and lilac to dark blue and red-purple, some of the flowers flecked with a darker color. There are no yellow English irises and none can be developed. The Massachusetts Bulletin 330 above referred to recommends the following from the many varieties tried:

> Duke of Clarence, pale blue
> Grand Lilas, pale lilac, flecked
> Grand Vainqueur, pale blue, flecked
> King of the Blues, dark blue
> Mont Blanc, white
> Prince of Wales, dark blue
> Royal Blue, dark blue, flecked
> Tricolor, pale lavender, mottled

To extend the range of color we might add Rosa Bonheur, white splashed with carmine, and Ruby, a deep reddish purple. However, the beginner may as well try whatever ones are procurable in America, even mixtures.

Raising English irises from seed is a job for the trade grower or the enthusiastic amateur and only advisable under very favorable conditions. Seed should be sown in autumn in beds or frames outdoors and the small resultant bulbs left until after the second summer before being moved to open ground. They should flower in the fourth season. One advantage of raising from seed is in the possibilities of improvement; another is that the flowers are pure in color and without the flecks found in many named varieties propagated by division. It is probable that English irises with mottling have a form of mosaic similar to the breaking of tulips. This does not affect their health.

English irises give us very attractive cut flowers. Either in bowls by themselves or with other flowers they have only to be seen to be desired. For long effectiveness in the house they should be cut just as the first flower is opening, as two in each head open in succession. For shipping they should be cut when the first bud shows considerable color, but before it opens. English irises cannot be forced.

SPANISH AND DUTCH IRISES

Far more important to the average gardener are the Spanish and Dutch irises. Their cultural needs are much more readily met than those of the English, and the bulbs are easier to get. In the case of the Dutch irises, the race is in process of much improvement.

In gardens the Spanish irises, variations of xiphium, long antedate the quite modern race of Dutch irises of somewhat similar appearance. The Dutch are larger and earlier. Forty years ago, when I grew large numbers of Spanish irises in my garden on the Stanford University campus, there were dozens of varieties to select in colors from pure white through pale and light to dark blues, yellows, bronzes and bicolors with white standards and colored falls. They were easy to grow, though our heavy adobe had to be drained and lightened to meet their needs for a light soil and freedom from wet feet. Their draw-backs from a garden standpoint are scant foliage and a short season of bloom. However, when planted close together (the bulbs about three inches deep and six inches apart) they are beautiful in early May and later. By inter-planting with summer annuals, their drying stems and dis-appearance in summer can be concealed. This practice is for California only. I also found them very useful for interplant-ing with daffodils which, being three inches deeper, did not compete for feeding; this arrangement also provided more foliage when the irises were in bloom and a second crop on the same ground.

Today Spanish irises have practically been replaced by the

related Dutch irises. However, to extend the season, they still have a value, as they come into flower after the Dutch are through. The number of varieties offered even in Dutch catalogues is now greatly reduced, but Cajanus, a large clear yellow and a tall grower, can be recommended, also British Queen or Queen Wilhelmina, both good whites; Excelsior, blue with yellow blotch; and the distinctive old Thunderbolt, a late-flowering smoky bronze.

Of all bulbous irises those with the trade name of Dutch are most important for garden use and cutting. During the early years of this century the Dutch firm of Van Tubergen made crosses of two xiphiums, Praecox, an early large-flowered blue, and Lusitanica, a large, early yellow. Possibly they also used the related filifolia from North Africa. Another Dutch firm, the de Graaffs, combined Praecox with commercial forms of Spanish irises. The resulting race has given many varieties in all the colors of the Spanish irises but with larger bulbs, stronger growth, and bigger flowers on taller stems, blooming on the average a couple of weeks earlier than the Spanish. Continuous breeding, including the use of the very early Moroccan species, tingitana, and the dark blue Fontanesii, is producing varieties still earlier and of greater vigor; new colors are appearing and the end is not in sight.

Commercial growing of Dutch irises is being taken up in America and has been reported along the Potomac, in the Carolinas, on Long Island, in Virginia, Illinois, Michigan, and Tennessee as well as in Oregon and Washington. Many of the varieties are being grown in the Pacific Northwest, and undoubtedly breeders there will contribute to their development. The Massachusetts bulletin already quoted states that even in the cold climate of Amherst, over the many experimental years which included some particularly tough winters, none of these irises was lost from freezing, although the only protection given was a covering of evergreen boughs. It is only fair to say that reports from many amateurs are less favorable, one difficulty with these plants being their insistence on producing their hard, narrow, scanty foliage before winter sets in. Protection with loose hay, leaves or other mulches seems pretty well to take care of this problem, as the foliage is not much bothered by frost. Often the drawback reported is not lack of bloom the first season after planting, but the tendency in some gardens, in the Chicago area for example, for bulbs to dwindle and eventually disappear. This is also true of some other bulbs (tulips and hyacinths, for example) and the annual expenditure—not a great one for Dutch iris bulbs are relatively cheap—seems as justified as for other expendable things.

The parents of the Dutch irises are native to climates of comparatively warm winters and hot dry summers. Give them, therefore, full sun wherever they are grown, and a light well-drained soil on the sandy side. After flowering, when they are going to rest and the foliage is dying down, provide all possible sunshine and drought. Plant the bulbs from three to four inches deep, depending on the heaviness of the soil and degree of winter cold; protection for the short, sparse winter foliage is important only in very cold climates. In spring the ground should be kept free of weeds or any other plant growth which would persist through the summer and keep the ground moist. Do not cut back the foliage until it has ripened. Lifting, grading, and dividing bulbs should be done only after stems and leaves have dried. Only the larger bulbs will flower the next year. Small offsets may as well be discarded, as they will take a year or more to grow to flowering size. Under favorable conditions it is not necessary to divide Dutch irises each year. Through indolence or oversight, or even malice aforethought, I often left some plantings undisturbed for years, and they developed into clumps from which several flower stems were produced.

Dutch irises may be raised from seed following the procedure described for the English. As they take three or four years to flower and it is highly unlikely that a mixed batch of seedlings will be up to the standard of even older and cheaper named varieties, this procedure can hardly be recommended.

The one disease which afflicts Dutch irises is mosaic, readily recognized by a striping of the foliage, stunted growth, and inferior flowers. Commercial growers ruthlessly discard in full growth any plant which shows signs of mosaic and are thus able to supply bulbs free of this disease when you get them. But if the garden contains old plantings in which mosaic is evident, or is in a place where conditions favor mosaic, in time the bulbs may become affected, and rigid roguing of those diseased is necessary to prevent complete infestation. Where there is much mosaic, just discard the whole stock and start over again. There is no danger that diseased bulbs will leave infection in the ground, as mosaic is transmitted only through aphis infesting plants in growth.

GARDEN USE AND SELECTION

In the garden, as their foliage is scanty and the bloom is all at the top, Dutch irises present problems somewhat similar to those of Amaryllis Belladonna. They are only effective when massed and should never be planted thinly along paths or the front of borders, but rather toward the back, with fore-grounds of other plants whose foliage will mask their sparse lower growth. In the herbaceous border, clumps of a single variety consisting of a dozen bulbs or more (the number depending on the scale of the border) will be found most effective. The clumps may be repeated at intervals, tying the whole together in their season of bloom. From experience I can recommend their interplanting with earlier spring-flowering bulbs, hyacinths or daffodils, to give a succession of bloom on the same ground. As the Dutch iris bulbs may be planted half the depth of daffodils, hyacinths, or tulips, they will not interfere in root growth with them.

Where recent plantings have been made of the tall bearded irises, bulbs of the Dutch iris may be scattered at intervals in the spaces between varieties, to be removed as the bearded irises thicken and cover the whole area in later years. When this is done varieties should be selected which do not bloom at the same time as the beardeds. Where conditions permit the easiest way is to plant Dutch irises in color groups by themselves in a place where they may be forgotten after flowering.

If Dutch irises are going to be used for cut flowers, for which purpose they are the best of all irises, the stems must not be cut to the ground but the lower leafage left to develop new flowering bulbs. (The trade practice is to consider the bulbs as expendable, cutting the stems right to the ground, and getting new bulbs each year.) The flowers are best cut as the first buds open, and as there are two in each head they last a long time.

In recent years commercial florists have developed a large business of growing the Dutch iris under glass for cut flowers,

since they are ideal for this purpose. As they may be shipped
when the first bud shows color they are rarely damaged in
transit. Amateurs with greenhouses may be interested in the
technique. Selection of varieties will naturally be based on the
time when flowers are desired, and later in this chapter will
be found a suggested list. The first early Wedgwood is the
most widely grown. Procure bulbs by mid-September and
plant in pots large enough to hold several, or in boxes preferably twice the depth of an ordinary flat. Fresh soil of not
too heavy character and without fresh manure in it is preferred. Plant the bulbs two inches deep and nearly that close
to one another if the flowers are to be cut. Plunge the containers to the ground level outdoors or in frames where they
may be left until in danger of hard freezing. By this time the
bulbs will have made some foliage and can be brought into
the greenhouse, which should be cool with a night temperature of from 45 to 50 degrees Fahrenheit, increasing five degrees in February, when most varieties may be brought into
flower. It is also possible to flower half a dozen bulbs in a
six-inch pot in the house. Place them close to the windows of
a room where similar temperatures can be maintained.

Amateurs can well afford to forget about the species and
varieties of xiphium from which the modern hybrids have
been raised. Like most wildflowers, they would be inferior
in size, vigor, and range of color. There are two possible exceptions, tingitana and Fontanesii. Whether the latter is a
separate species or only a late mountain form of tingitana,
the botanists do not seem to have decided yet. Iris tingitana,
which grows wild around Tangiers on the African side of
the Straits of Gibraltar, bears a fine big precocious sky-blue
flower with tall stems. I have induced it to bloom in central

California but after the first year it produced only foliage, as we lack the intense summer heat needed to ripen it properly. Gardeners in the hotter, drier parts of southern California and Arizona might have more success with it outdoors. Thus far its main value has been as the parent of Wedgwood, the earliest of the Dutch irises and a not dissimilar flower. Iris Fontanesi can only rarely be obtained in the trade, even in Europe. Years ago a French friend sent me a few bulbs which grew well here. It proved to be a dark velvety purple, and from crossing it with a blue Dutch iris my neighbor Carl Salbach raised the darkest, richest Dutch iris I have yet seen. It was introduced by the Oregon Bulb Farms as National Velvet.

So many really good Dutch irises have been introduced that no one can make a list which would be everybody's choice. I have attempted in the following lists to suggest (1) a good standard collection, one or two of each color, and (2) a collection of greatly improved novelties recently introduced to the American trade.

(1) *Some Other Standard Varieties*

> Huchtenburg, standards cream, falls yellow
> Imperator, fine deep blue
> Jacob De Wit, early blue
> Lilac Queen, white standards, lilac falls
> Poggenbeek, dark blue
> Wedgwood, early pale blue
> White Excelsior, pure white
> Yellow Queen, golden yellow

(2) *Some Recent Novelties*

> Aviator, purple-blue with orange spot
> Belle Jaune, deep golden yellow
> Blue Champion, large deep blue
> Blue Pearl, deep violet, wonderful color

Harmony, standards blue, falls yellow
Jeanne d'Arc, large, tall, creamy white
King Mauve, distinct orchid color
Lemon Queen, primrose and chrome yellow
National Velvet, deep purple
Orange King, deep color
Princess Irene, cream with orange blotch
White Pearl, large, pure white

To these novelties might be added Bronze Beauty, Bronze Queen, or Le Mogol, all of which bring into the Dutch irises the odd, smoky tints of the old Spanish iris Thunderbolt, but most gardeners do not want too many of these somber blends.

CHAPTER FOUR

Crested Irises

There is a small group of iris species more closely related to the bearded than to the beardless irises. All are distinguished by a linear crest at the base of the falls; botanically they are known as the evansias. From a garden standpoint several crested irises have proved satisfactory and are valued because of the particular situations in which they may be used. As a group they thrive under shadier conditions than other irises. Iris cristata is the only one native to America; the other evansias—gracilipes, tectorum, and japonica—are imports from Japan or China.

OUR NATIVE CRISTATA

Iris cristata is a miniature species, best adapted to rock gardening or to naturalization. Its small rhizomes bear rather broad leaves and make an attractive green carpet as background for the lovely little lavender flowers with golden crests. While cristata adapts itself to an astonishing variety of locations, its preference is for afternoon shade, good drainage, and a gravelly soil containing considerable humus, for it grows wild under conditions of cool damp mossy soil and summer moisture.

Success in garden culture of cristata is reported as far north as Montreal in eastern Canada and Vancouver Island in the

Northwest; it is of course happy in the southeastern states where it is native, and is grown right across the continent to California. In my own garden near San Francisco, it is planted in a rocky ledge where through the summer it gets moisture from the watering of an adjacent piece of lawn. Here it has persisted for years with no special care and flow-

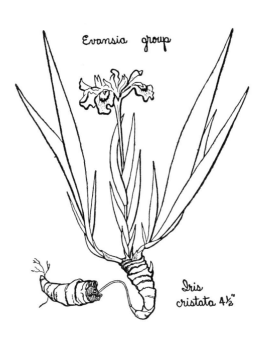

Evansia group

Iris cristata 4½"

ers freely every April. It is doubtful however whether this species would be successful in the deep South or in the arid parts of the Southwest, with their baking summer sun. Around the Great Lakes and particularly north of Lake Huron a variety of cristata called lacustris is found in great quantities, but it is less beautiful and less adaptable than cristata to varying conditions.

Increase of cristata is by the removal of the new growth, but the thinning out of the slender greenish rhizome, or any transplanting, is best done immediately following flowering, when new roots are produced. After early summer there is no new growth, and propagation or transplanting in autumn is generally unsuccessful as the plants fail to make growth necessary to establish them. One successful grower in northern New Jersey however reports good results from divisions made before blooming in spring and for some time afterwards in summer.

JAPANESE IMPORTS

Iris gracilipes from the woodlands of Japan likes about the same conditions as cristata. From its thin, grasslike foliage slender stems rise to a height of eight or ten inches, branched so that each will carry several of the small lavender flowers, which are about an inch across. It is not quite so tough as our native crested iris, will not thrive in a hot dry place, and sometimes suffers from the heaving of alternate thawing and freezing in early spring. Give it a moist, drained soil with humus or leaf mold, and do not ask it to endure hot afternoon sun. The best time for dividing and increasing gracilipes is in spring or summer when growth is active, never in autumn, as it seems unable to establish itself then. In gardens, gracilipes could be grown almost as widely as cristata, yet it seems relatively little known.

Originally a native of China, Iris tectorum derives its name "roof iris" from being grown on the ridges of thatched roofs in Japan. This location possibly is responsible for the impression that it is a sun-loving and drought-enduring species, but it does not prove so in American or English gardens, where tectorum is happiest with shade half the day. Its preference in soils is for a rich humus mixture on the acid rather than the alkaline side. It grows well from the Atlantic to the Pacific Coast, with the greatest ease apparently in the Southeast; it does well also in Nashville, Macon, Shreveport, and on the Pacific Coast from central California north. Both successes and failures occur in the same areas and even when this iris has been moved from one location to another in the same garden. In the colder parts of Canada and in the north central states it is apt to be short-lived and not floriferous.

Tectorum has a shallow-rooting rhizome with the reputation of quickly exhausting the soil, which should therefore be well enriched yearly. This, of course, may only delay the necessity of replanting as soon as flowering becomes sparse. Replanting is perhaps best done every two or three years, in July or August, though one of the most successful growers sets out new plantings in spring, summer, or fall, and the time does not seem to make any difference. Iris tectorum is easily raised from seed, which germinates quickly, the young plants often giving flowers in their second year.

The typical tectorum has rather broad, ribbed leaves which eventually grow a foot or more long. The stems with their blooms of purple-blue, almost flat, push up just above the foliage. There is also a pure white form which is often considered more attractive than the blue. Under favorable conditions it seems to be equally happy, but over the country at large the white form has proved more delicate than the blue and has shown a greater tendency to die out at an early age. Clumps of Iris tectorum are very effective in larger rock gardens and bordering paths in partial shade, but the most effective planting I have seen was at the base of a house wall in a quite warm position, where it was of course necessary to water occasionally through the summer.

Many years ago Sir Michael Foster succeeded in crossing one of the forms of Iris pallida with tectorum. The resulting hybrid, named Paltec, greatly resembles tectorum and in some gardens, because of easier culture, it has been found a satisfactory substitute. Oliver Twist, another tectorum seedling of ranker growth, is said to succeed better than its parent in a garden in Ventura, California.

JAPONICAS AND HYBRIDS

Iris japonica, sometimes also called I. fimbriata, is the most distinctive and beautiful of the crested irises. From fans of thin, bright evergreen foliage it sends up two-foot widely branched stems which bear over several weeks a succession of somewhat fugitive but lovely pale lavender flowers, fringed, and with orange crests. A single stem will bear dozens of blooms, so light and airy and so like orchids that this particular species is often referred to as the "orchid" iris. It is quite widely grown in California, where it is perfectly hardy all along the coast.

Japonica is not in the least demanding as to soil, though its preferences are for one that is not too heavy and that contains humus and leaf mold. In contrast with almost all other irises, it succeeds far better in considerable shade than in sunlight and often will be found growing luxuriantly in the dappled shade of overhanging trees. Unfortunately japonica cannot be grown outdoors in very cold climates, but all along the

Pacific Coast and through the southern states it is well worth trying.

Walter Marx wrote me that he formerly grew japonica in eastern Oregon, where hot dry summers and zero temperatures in winter were usual. Conditions were otherwise favorable as it was planted under oaks in loamy soil acidified by rotted oak leaves. In his present garden at Boring, not far from Portland in western Oregon, he finds it of unquestionable hardiness, standing temperatures from five to ten degrees above zero without damage. However, in colder climates of the Atlantic Coast and the Middle West japonica must be grown indoors, where it flowers well under glass or in a pot or box near a window. A real asset in early spring, it is a decorative plant with beautiful flowers. (In England a hardier form of japonica is offered by nurserymen under the name Ledger's Variety, but I have not heard of this being grown in America.)

Closely related to japonica is the similar species Iris Wattii, which has the peculiar habit of throwing up its leaved flower stems in the year preceding flowering. In growth it suggests a bamboo with a fan of leaves two or three feet above the ground. From this the much branched flower spikes appear, the flowers themselves being paler than in japonica, almost white. This species is harder to grow than japonica in cold climates because of damage to the flower stem.

J. N. Giridlian in Arcadia, California has raised from a cross of japonica and Wattii a beautiful hybrid, Nada, and from Nada a further introduction called Darjeeling. These make lovely garden plants, well-established clumps producing numerous stems with hundreds of butterflylike blooms, most attractive in the garden and plentiful for cutting.

Adventurous gardeners interested in species should try members of this group if their local temperature does not drop below zero. The best chance of success will lie in securing rhizomes in late spring or early summer after flowering and establishing them before cold weather, under the favored soil and shade conditions.

CHAPTER FIVE

Beardless Irises of America

The native irises of North America are all beardless.
Except for the Pacific Coast group, nearly all grow
naturally under wet conditions, though most of them stand
drought in summer. They comprise several species of secondary garden value common east and north of the Mississippi River; the Louisiana group of three related species and
a wonderful series of apparently natural hybrids; a varying
species native to the Rocky Mountain region, with a California relative; and a Pacific Coast series second only to the
Louisiana group in present and potential value.

Iris setosa is the species that once must have extended clear
across the continent from Alaska to Labrador. The forms
surviving today in Labrador, on the Gaspé Peninsula, and in
northern Maine are dwarfer and less varied than the Alaskan
remnants of the species. They make satisfactory ornamental
garden plants, and though their natural habitat is very wet,
adapt themselves to garden culture with no more water than
most herbaceous plants need. They form clumps of broad
foliage shorter than the stems, which carry many light purplish blue flowers, often veined darker. The color effect
comes from the falls, the standards being quite inconspicuous.

THE COMMON FLAG AND OTHER NATIVES
OF THE EAST

Iris versicolor or the common flag of eastern marshes is a taller, more lax-growing iris than setosa, with larger, looser flowers of varying shades. Generally a blue-purple with lines and a little yellow at the base of the falls, it shows some variation: the variety kermesina is a rich red-purple. Like its closest relative, Iris Pseudacorus of European marshes and streams, versicolor can easily be naturalized under similar conditions or grown as a border plant, doing quite well with only moderate summer moisture. In gardens of arid summers it must be watered; a location near the lawn is an easy way to insure periodic moistening.

Iris virginica which takes up where versicolor leaves off, extending from Ohio and Illinois down into and beyond the Mississippi Valley, is one of the species widely seen in Louisiana. There it varies sufficiently to provide attractive garden forms, but does not interbreed with the other native species. (Iris carolina and I. Shrevei are now considered as merely varieties of virginica.)

Iris virginica has grand, glossy foliage two feet or more high and slender branched two- to three-foot flower stalks. The dominant color is lavender, often with darker veining. Its garden use is much like that of versicolor, though selected forms of greater value may perhaps be obtained.

Iris verna is the little dwarf found wild in the southern Appalachians in patches where there is some shade and moist peaty soil. Its blue-lilac flowers, with an orange band on the falls suggesting those of the pumila irises, grow on ten-inch stems above the shorter foliage. It is less amenable to cultivation than most species, though worth trying where you have a half-shady nook with acid soil and moisture throughout the summer. In my own garden it does not so far appear happy, even when grown with other moisture- and shade-loving species.

Iris prismatica is an American species of the sibirica group, which grows wild among pines in the southern mountains and under bog conditions along the coastal plain. It is not unlike a small sibirica in appearance, but its eighteen-inch stems are more solid. The flowers vary from violet to nearly blue. It is best raised from seed, as collected plants move with difficulty and only late in the season.

LOUISIANA IRISES UNDER CULTURE

The most thrilling event in iris history was the discovery of great numbers of plants growing in the swamps and bayous of southeastern Louisiana. After much controversy, Iris fulva, I. foliosa, and I. giganticærulea are now generally accepted as the only certain species in what botanists are now calling the hexagona subsection. Tentatively, at least, the rest are assumed to be varieties of these three or their natural hybrids. The first discoveries were made around New Orleans. Later plants were found farther west, mostly around Lafayette.

The finer forms, selected by interested amateurs and taken into cultivation, have added beautiful pure whites, yellows, pinks, reds, and purples, as well as an almost complete range of blues. Some of these collected varieties are reputed shy blooming, but from them it will be possible to develop a strictly garden race of water-loving irises. These may even-

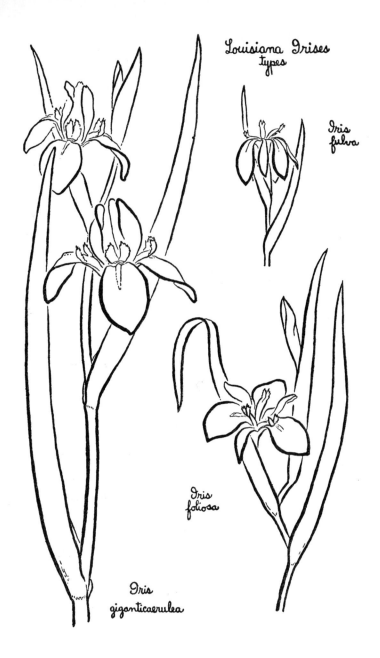

Louisiana Irises
types

Iris
fulva

Iris
foliosa

Iris
giganticaerulea

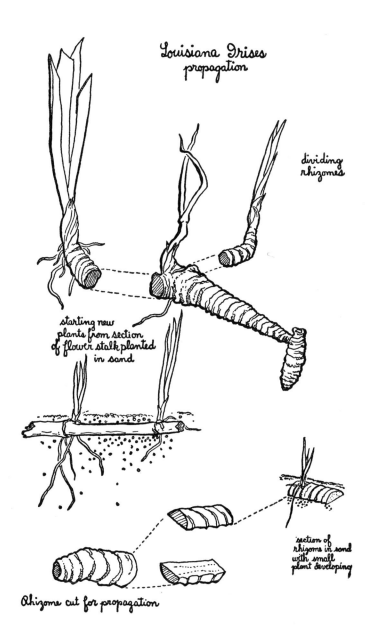

Louisiana Irises
propagation

dividing
rhizomes

starting new
plants from section
of flower stalk planted
in sand

section of
rhizome in sand
with small
plant developing

Rhizome cut for propagation

tually prove superior to the Japanese in form and color. They have a grace which the often rather stiff, heavy modern forms of Iris Kaempferi lack.

For gardens on the coastal plain and in states along the Gulf of Mexico where tall bearded irises are unsuccessful, Louisiana irises will be the first of the family in importance. The extraordinary thing about them is their climatic tolerance. With only reasonable care as to winter covering, they grow in places as cold as New England, and with attention to adequate watering during their season of growth, they are quite happy in the gardens of southern California, where summer rain is regarded as an accident.

Iris fulva, easily identified by its flowers of terra-cotta color, is native also in Georgia, Texas, Arkansas, and in the Mississippi Valley as far north as Ohio and Illinois. It is not effective in the garden since the flowers, produced from the axils of the leaves on stems about two feet high, are small and droop in a depressing way. This species is not difficult to grow, provided it is given plenty of moisture until after flowering and a fair amount of water throughout the summer.

Iris foliosa, the smallest and shortest of the Louisiana species, thrives in deposits laid down by Ol' Man River west of the present Mississippi riverbed. Like fulva, it has some scattered distribution in neighboring states. It has beautiful foliage and relatively short zigzag stems so that the blue-violet flowers borne in the axils are often hidden by the leaves.

Iris giganticærulea is the tallest of the three, with leaves three feet or slightly more in height and a stout nearly straight flower stalk always overtopping the foliage. The dominant color is columbine blue, but there is considerable variation from pure white through many shades of blue.

Growing naturally under bog conditions or along the margin of slow-moving bayous, the Louisiana irises do well when planted in similar situations, but they are also content in gardens where soil, fertilization, and water meet the needs of growing vegetables. They prefer a neutral or slightly acid soil, not too light, and with much humus. If this is not found in the garden, excavate the soil at least a foot and fill in with good garden soil mixed with manure and leaf mold. Filtered shade is desirable in warmer climates, but is unnecessary in the North where all three species thrive in full sun. The fleshy rhizomes should be planted just below the surface and at some distance apart if the planting is to remain for some years. However, as these irises like to travel and enjoy new soil and good feeding, it is common practice to replant about every three years, either after blooming or in late summer or autumn.

Carl Milliken told me that he obtained better growth the first year by giving rhizomes received from the South in late summer a few weeks in a wet sand bed to induce root growth before planting them out in his garden at Arcadia, California. If the bed has been depressed slightly it can be flooded occasionally through the growing season, the water being tapered off after flowering, but these irises so easily adapt themselves to gardens that they are well worth growing anywhere outside of extremely arid areas.

PROPAGATION AND BREEDING

Increase of varieties is by vegetative propagation, mainly division of the rhizomes. This is quite rapid, as after blooming new rhizomes will be produced on each side of the stalk and these will flower the following year. Propagation by rhizome separation may be done at any replanting time, but there is speedier multiplication immediately after flowering. Where many plants of a very desirable variety are wanted in a short time, rhizome cuttings may be made: that is, the older part of the rhizome back of the growing end may be removed and cut into sections a couple of inches long and these planted and kept moist in a cool location. From the buds which lie dormant at the ring scars new shoots will develop. When these have enough roots to take care of themselves they should be removed and planted in the garden.

Breeders, still mainly Louisiana amateurs, raise new varieties from seed, sometimes self-set seed from selected forms, more often obtained by cross-fertilization. Because the Louisiana irises are readily self-fertilized, the stamens of the flower to be used as seed-bearer should be removed before the flower is fully open and the pollen becomes powdery. By then the stigma is ready for fertilization and the desired pollen from another flower can be placed on it. Careful breeders advise covering the fertilized flower with a muslin or other protective bag to prevent later accidental pollination.

The tendency of the seed to lie dormant was for some time a problem, but Dr. George Arcenaux found that by removing the seed from the pod when approximately a third to a half of its surface was still green and immediately planting it, sixty to ninety per cent germination resulted in the following fall and winter. Seeds may be planted either in beds of half and half sand and garden soil or in deep cans, in either case covered with an inch of soil. When the seedlings are three or four inches high, they should be moved into the bed where they will flower and spaced not less than a foot apart.

SELECTION FOR GARDENS AND INDOORS

Long before the present interest in the Louisiana irises, crosses were made of the small typical form of Iris fulva and foliosa. The resultant hybrids, all good garden plants with red-purple flowers, have been widely grown. Three of these are Fulvala, Dorothea K. Williamson, and Cacique. Afterward came the more important work of the late T. A. Washington of Nashville, who from material largely collected in Mississippi raised a series of hybrids in a pleasing range of color. These, later put into commerce by a New England grower, included such varieties as Valbancha, orchid pink; Mary Love, pink lavender; Martha Washington, old rose; and Rosanna Holt, pansy purple. However, we are most concerned with the discovery in the swamps of Louisiana around New Orleans of a great variety of forms—the giant Abbeville reds, possibly entitled to specific rank, the variations on the fine tall giganticærulea, the natural hybrids between these, and the still later and often finer hybrids raised by Louisiana breeders. It is all but impossible in the present state of dissemination to list the best varieties; I am therefore giving the names of those added to my own garden on the advice of specialists and from my own observation of the good collection which I saw in flower in southern California—Magnoliapetal, white; Cajan Joyeuse, bright rose; Caroline Dormon, pale yellow and rose red; David Fischer, light orchid; Bayou Vermilion, red; and Haile Selassie, deep red. A few newer varieties which have been widely recommended are the white Barbara Elaine Taylor and Her Highness (one of the finest

of the collected whites); the blue Flat Top and Ruth Holley-
man; the purple Beau Geste, Violet Ray and The Kahn; the
yellow Dixie Debutante (yellows are still rare); and the pink
and rose varieties Peggy Mac, Bayou Sunset and Wheelhorse.
Cherry Bounce, Caddo and Sybil Sample are various shades
of red.

Of the whole family these Louisiana irises are the most
beautiful for cut-flower arrangements. Their fine green foliage, the occurrence of the flowers in the nodes of the graceful
stems, and the succession of blooms in each head all contribute to their attractiveness indoors. Add to this a wonderful
range of colors including nearly pure blues, and their light
and informal character, and you discover in this group materials for indoor decoration unequaled in the stiffer spurias
and Dutch irises favored by most florists.

IRIS MISSOURIENSIS

Iris missouriensis always grows wild in ground which is
very wet in spring, but dries out pretty completely in summer. Such conditions it finds from the upper reaches of the
Missouri River through the Great Basin and the Rocky
Mountains; it grows as far south as Tulare County and the
San Bernardino Mountains and as far north as Washington.
As it varies considerably from place to place, some botanists
have distinguished as species local variations of this species,
one of the two in series Longipetalae.

Typically missouriensis throws up stems a couple of feet,
well above the deciduous foliage, with flowers white or pale
blue and much darker veining. Pure whites have been found
and offered by one Colorado nursery. A pleasant plant of
easy culture, it is not remarkable as its coloring is common

among beardless irises. It can be grown almost anywhere and is very hardy.

PACIFIC COAST NATIVES

The beautiful series of irises found along the West Coast is often referred to rather narrowly as the "California" series. First to come to mind is Iris longipetala (the second species in the series Longipetalae) not for its prime importance but because it stands out distinctly from other natives. It is so much like missouriensis that it will not surprise the gardener to find it a California relative of that species, but of shorter stature, with heavily blue-lined white flowers that barely appear above the evergreen leaves.

Found wild from San Francisco southward to Monterey in marshy ground that dries out in summer, longipetala takes kindly to the garden, transplants or divides more easily than other Pacific Coast natives, but like them can be raised from seed. Recently I put out a batch of seedling on a piece of dry hillside which never remains wet even in winter, and yet all are flourishing.

Iris Hartwegii, a native of the pine forests of the Sierra Nevada frequently seen in the Yosemite Valley, has flowers of creamy yellow with darker lines. Another form occurring in the San Bernardino Range produces lavender and purple flowers. Less noticeable and consequently less grown than characteristic species of the coast, it has been used by English breeders in crossing with some of the sibirica group such as chrysographes. The lovely deep purple hybrid called Chrysowegii has flowered in my garden.

The series of relatively low-growing irises comprising Douglasiana, tenax, bracteata, innominata, and some minor species of the West Coast is second only to the Louisiana natives; the values of the two groups are so different that no real competition exists. Even when collected from the wild, these species will adapt themselves quickly to cultivation, bearing flowers of charm and beauty in a wide color range most desirable in the garden and for cutting.

No flaunting beauties, these natives of central and northern California, Oregon, and Washington can be grown successfully in British Columbia and can adapt themselves to southern gardens away from the hot, moist coastal plain. Adventurous amateurs have flowered them with cold frame or other protection as far north as Quebec, but conditions are less favorable for them in the Great Lakes area, the Prairie States, or the Rocky Mountain region.

Even within certain species there is great variation in growth, size and color of flowers, and height of stem, and the tendency for natural hybrids to occur where different species overlap in nature is confusing. Happily the Rancho Santa Ana Botanic Garden, has undertaken a genetic study of this series. Part I of A Revision of the Pacific Coast Irises by Dr. Lee W. Lenz was published in Aliso, Vol. 4, No. 1, April 1958.

Iris Douglasiana is a robust evergreen species growing in dense tufts often in moist open woods and in quite heavy soil. The flower stems rising above abundant foliage are sometimes branched, and the heads carry two or three buds, so that a clump remains in flower a long time. Forms collected in one area are short and compact; elsewhere growth may be so rampant as to seem coarse. The flowers also vary considerably in size and the color range is extraordinary, from pure white through cream and yellow, or from pale

Pacific Coast
species

Iris
longipetala
30"

Iris
Douglasiana
20"

Iris
innominata
14"

lavender and pink to rich blue-purple; many have a light ground with a darker suffusion toward the center of the fall which adds interest to their beauty.

It is strange that Douglasiana is not more widely grown in gardens of the Pacific Coast and anywhere else where it will thrive, as it is easily domesticated. Like all the native irises of this series, it wants a neutral or somewhat acid soil and certainly enjoys humus and leaf mold. However, in a number of gardens it is thriving to my knowledge under quite ordinary conditions. Unquestionably it will stand considerable shade and, except along the cool foggy coast, will be happier if it does not have full sunshine all day. Grown in patches on level ground or anywhere in the less formal parts of the garden to which its woodsy character is adapted, it is at home and effective. An extensive planting of Douglasiana in a park in Piedmont near Oakland has for many years been giving a wonderful, sylvan effect every March and April. Many years ago, I planted this iris on a very steep bank to hold the soil; year after year it blooms so generously as to excite interest of all visitors.

A more northerly species not found wild in California is Iris tenax, native to western Oregon and Washington. It is less robust, less rampant, daintier in growth than Douglasiana; its tufts of lighter green foliage are looser and the flowers are borne singly on stems varying from six to ten inches. Frequently found in dry open woods, tenax likes rather loose soil adapted to its slender, stringy rhizomes. In Oregon it is reputed to improve under cultivation, but in California it has not generally proved as easy as the more vigorous Douglasiana. The prevailing color is lavender, but specialists have gathered pure whites, creamy tints, pearl gray, orchid, blue, and purple, and frequently attractive patterns of more than one color. This is an iris for the rock garden, and deserves a choicer place than Douglasiana.

Iris Gormanii from the Coast Range of Oregon is not now considered distinct from the species I. tenax. The blossoms are a soft yellow, almost apricot, in one plant given me by a friend. This iris has established itself in a half-shady location on the edge of some pines which annually mulch it with needles; it is lovely.

Iris innominata was discovered only in 1928 and christened shortly afterward. In the inaccessible rugged mountains of southwest Oregon where it grows wild the winters are cold with a good deal of snow, and summers are hot and dry. The soil is rocky and coarse under covering forests of fir and pine. However, innominata does not insist upon such rigors. Conditions are quite different around San Francisco Bay where we have no great winter cold, no snow, and cool foggy summers, and where the soil is relatively heavy though neutral or acid; yet this iris adapts itself perfectly to such situations. In several Berkeley gardens where it flourishes, innominata is invariably acclaimed the most charming of little irises and the greatest addition in our time to the list of easily grown plants for rock gardens. The foliage is dark green and grassy but heavy in texture and evergreen. In a couple of years low tufty clumps can be developed from seed or divisions with many flowers on stems varying from three to ten inches, depending on the particular form. The typical and most popular color is pure golden yellow; often the yellows are heavily lined with a deeper shade or even with brown. In recent years collectors have found many different color forms—bright violet and orchid, yellows with so much brown in the falls that they suggest variegatas, and even white grounds with orchid or red venation.

These three species—Douglasiana, tenax, and innominata —are the really important Pacific Coast irises for our gardens. In nature where they grow together lovely natural hybrids have resulted, and as collectors gather fine forms and inter-breed them, a garden race of the greatest value will doubt-less be developed. Such a race will have uses quite different from those of the bearded irises or of the swamp-loving spe-cies.

I have always regarded the Pacific Coast irises as best planted by themselves in drifts, but an association seen in the beautiful garden of Dr. Matthew C. Riddle in Portland, Oregon, is new and provides one solution for the path or border of tall bearded iris. He uses Iris innominata in many lovely colors as an informal edging for beds of the tall beardeds; low, graceful growth of innominata breaks the stiff line of the taller foliage and brings color right down to the lawn. Many pleasing combinations of very different irises are possible in climates where innominata can be grown. For larger beds or borders Iris Douglasiana might be similarly used with the beardeds.

Of secondary importance, yet desirable for variety's sake are such species as Iris macrosiphon, I. bracteata, and I. tenuis. A native of California and Oregon, chiefly in the coast ranges, macrosiphon has narrow foliage a foot or more high. The flower stems measure only two or three inches, though the long perianth tube lifts them up to a height of five or six inches. The flowers of blue and red-purple are not conspicuous in the garden, as they are set low in the foliage. Iris chrysophylla is merely a variety of macrosiphon.

Iris bracteata grows wild in the oak and pine forests of southwestern Oregon. Its leathery bractlike leaves, glossy above and dull underneath, are produced in scanty tufts at the ends of slender creeping rhizomes. The foliage overtops the yellow flowers with brownish purple veins, which are carried on stems about eight inches high.

Iris tenuis, found mostly in the Clackamas area of north central Oregon is excluded from the series Californicae in the Lenz 1958 reclassification. In cultivation, its rather casual growth is reported to become more compact, forming fine floriferous clumps with creamy white flowers, veined purple with a yellow blotch. Although I have had no experience with this rarer species in California, both macrosiphon and bracteata have adapted themselves very well in our garden.

PROPAGATION BY DIVISION AND SEED

If the Pacific Coast irises were common in nurseries they would be widely grown in gardens. Most gardeners like to start with plants and these irises do not lend themselves to such distribution. They resent transplanting at any time or division, except when they are beginning to make new root growth. A dealer in Washington has found them amenable to shipping in autumn possibly because plants never dry out as much in the north.

The named varieties Agnes James, Amiguta, Golden Nymph, Orchid Sprite and Santa Ana are available from this nursery. A California nursery offers the new Douglasiana hybrids of Dr. Roswell H. Johnson, as well as the Richard Luhrsen originations.

Fred De Forest of Canby, Oregon, reports that divisions

planted in rows and frequently separated have a vigor of root growth under nursery culture which is not obtainable from offsets of old clumps not so grown. Possibly this procedure or establishing divisions in gallon cans in accordance with California practice for many herbaceous plants will facilitate distribution and propagation of special selections or named varieties, very few of which now exist. Propagation is certainly most satisfactory in spring—this may be January in California or much later in colder climates—when, if newer growths are removed from the outside of clumps just before new roots are produced, they will rapidly re-establish themselves and eventually grow into fine plants. If they are kept out of the ground for any length of time for shipping or other reasons care must be taken that they do not dry out.

It is easier to raise all these irises from seed which is abundantly produced and remains viable for some years. The best procedure is to sow in beds or seed frames, or in pots if only a few plants are wanted, using a friable or sandy soil and covering the seed at least half an inch deep. Preferably this is done in autumn outdoors. Germination will be assisted by winter rains and frost though it does not occur until early spring at about the same time established plants begin to make new growth.

The little seedlings may be left in the frames or beds, watered all summer, and planted out the following autumn. Under this treatment not many can be expected to flower the spring after germination. The proportion can be greatly increased and better plants for setting out obtained if in late spring or early summer the seedlings are pricked out and replanted two or three inches apart in beds of good soil kept well watered and cultivated through the summer. Such plants may go into the garden either in autumn or early spring.

All these Pacific Coast irises are among the most attractive and dainty flowers for cutting in the whole family. With their varying sizes and lengths of stem, they make pleasing table decoration and arrangements of all kinds.

CHAPTER SIX

Beardless Irises from the Old World

All the wild parents of our bearded and bulbous irises came originally from Asia and Europe and the African shore of the Mediterranean. The Old World likewise supplies the very best beardless irises for garden purposes along with some species of minor importance. The most important groups are the Siberians, the Japanese irises and the spurias. Besides these, we owe to the Old World several distinctive individual species.

While the modern Siberian beardless irises lack the gorgeousness of the tall bearded species, a good case can still be made for them as the members of the family best adapted to culture in the colder climates of North America. For hardy herbaceous borders and planting in wet ground, as well as for their delightful butterflylike flowers, they are unsurpassed. The wild Iris sibirica grows in wet meadows through much of central Europe. It has a fibrous root system and narrow grassy foliage from which so many tall hollow flower stems emerge in early summer that in season each clump is completely crowned with blue or white flowers.

A very close relative, Iris orientalis, is native to much of northeastern Asia. It differs from sibirica in somewhat broader foliage and shorter flower stems, which appear to rise above the somewhat drooping leafage. This species can also be identified by the spathes, which are often suffused with red-purple. The flowers are larger than those of sibirica, typically of a rich blue-purple, paling to white in the center of the falls. There is also a white form of orientalis grown under the name Snow Queen.

DOMESTICATED SIBERIANS

While both sibirica and orientalis are attractive garden plants, the crosses between them with perhaps some slight interbreeding of related species have given us a garden race far superior to the parents. The flowers are larger and have a wider color range; there are now pure whites taller than Snow Queen and a whole series of blues from the very palest through clear, darker shades to purple-blues and violet. Recent breeding has also developed varieties with reddish flowers.

Among the many irises I grew in Montreal during the years I lived there none were so completely dependable or so rewarding. Yet Siberian irises are quite successful right across the continent and all through the Pacific Northwest. They can be grown wherever winters are mild, but I have never seen them so luxuriant or anything like so floriferous as where the winters are cold. They are of questionable value in those parts of the South where bearded irises do not succeed, and only where exceptional conditions have been provided do they survive in the arid areas of the Southwest; one very good iris grower in Albuquerque reports that they are not happy under his quite typical conditions of long hot dry summers.

Always give Siberians a sunny situation. They will of

course stand a great deal of water, particularly in spring and summer but they are surprisingly able to adapt themselves to ordinary garden conditions and get along with the same amount of moisture as most hardy herbaceous plants. Planting, and this includes division of old clumps, is best done in late summer or early autumn. In warmer areas October will be better. These irises can also be moved in early spring, but with somewhat less success. They do not enjoy disturbance and as the full effect of flowering comes only with clumps which are well established, they should remain undisturbed for years. They may be thinned or divisions removed to start new plantings by simply chiseling out sections from the margins of the spreading clumps. Pieces should be taken which have half a dozen or more shoots rather than single offsets. If a rich, somewhat heavy soil is provided, they will not need fertilizing until the clumps are large, when a mulch of old manure will be of great assistance.

Siberian irises may also be raised from seed sown in autumn in boxes outdoors, from which the seedlings will have to be transplanted into the open ground the following spring; or under favorable conditions, the seed may even be sown in the ground a couple of inches apart and the plants allowed to bloom without moving. By either method a good proportion will flower the second year, when the best ones may be selected for garden display. While some variation will be found in any batch of seedlings from chance pods, hand pollination should be used where it is desired to combine the qualities of the parents. In the case of the Siberians as with many beardless species, self-pollination so readily occurs in an early stage that the careful breeder must open the flower and remove the anthers before the pollen appears.

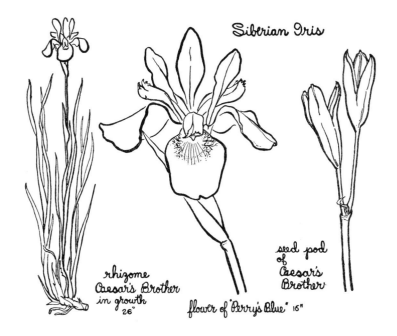

Siberian Iris

rhizome
Caesar's Brother
in growth
26"

seed pod
of
Caesar's
Brother

flower of "Perry's Blue" 16"

USEFUL GARDEN VARIETIES

The greatest value of Siberians is in the hardy herbaceous border, where, without any special provision for extra watering, they thrive amazingly under the same conditions as the other plants. Clumps of a single variety planted at intervals in the middle areas will give delightful airy effects. While the whites, dark blues, and the newer reds are useful for variety, it is those with pale or pure blue flowers, like Perry's Blue and Gatineau, that charm us with their rather rare color. Where a pool is a feature of the garden, there are no better irises for planting along the margin. In more informal places near a stream or larger body of water, the shores offer a wonderful opportunity for mass effects with Siberian irises. In California it is good practice to assemble them in a part of the garden such as on the edge of a lawn which is watered through the rainless summer. Where there is a pond they can be just as effectively used as in colder climates and will be fairly floriferous, judging by their presence in the Japanese Tea Garden in Golden Gate Park in San Francisco. They are not aquatic plants, however, and should not be submerged in water or covered with it when dormant in winter.

The older varieties of Siberians, many of them still worth growing, were, almost wholly by breeders in the colder eastern states (Mrs. Frances Cleveland, the Kelloggs, Fred R. Whitney, and others) and by Canadians (Cleveland Morgan in Montreal and Isabella Preston in Ottawa). So little breeding has been done in recent years that the Morgan Award has been inactivated. F. W. Cassebeer's beautiful wide-petaled White Swirl, a great advance in this breeding, stands almost alone.

The following suggested list is arranged by color. (For full descriptions consult dealers' catalogues.)

White
    Rimouski
    Snow Crest
    White Swirl
Blue
    Cool Spring
    Gatineau
    Mountain Lake
    Perry's Blue

Purple
    Caesar's Brother
    Royal Ensign
    Tropic Night
    Tycoon
Reddish
    Eric the Red
    Helen Astor

Iris Delavayi, introduced fairly recently from the swamps of western China, is taller and stronger than the typical sibirica, with an even greater liking for a rich moist soil. Though not so effective a garden plant as the Siberian irises, it is valuable for use under similar conditions as its blue- or red-purple flowers follow the Siberians in season. The activities of English breeders in crossing this vigorous species with related Asiatic species may produce better and more distinctive garden hybrids.

Among the other minor members of the Siberian group are three relatively late introductions from western China—Iris chrysographes, I. Forrestii, and I. Wilsonii. These are available in America and well worth growing if you can meet their more exacting requirements for a rich humus soil and moisture throughout the summer. They are happiest in the damp climates of coastal Oregon, Washington, and British Columbia. All three are more temperamental than the Siberian irises, but enthusiasts have succeeded with them and value them for their different colors. Years ago I failed with them in a warm westward-facing garden in California, but now in my cooler garden I am trying them again under conditions suitable for the Louisiana irises. Hybrids are being raised within these varieties—Chrysoforrestii is one example—and there are combinations even with the California species: the English introduction Margot Holmes is claimed as a hybrid of chrysographes and tenax, and Chrysowegii as a combination of chrysographes and Hartwegii.

Iris chrysographes is a really lovely thing, rather like a shorter Siberian, its rich red-purple velvety falls veined with gold. There is a variety rubella, without markings. In cold climates this species is best divided and replanted in early autumn so that it may get established before winter. It is readily raised from seed and bloom may be expected the second year. Iris Forrestii in foliage and habit suggests a dwarf form of the Siberian iris, its value being that its bright yellow flowers veined with brown bring a new color into this section. Wilsonii is less desirable as the flower is of a paler yellow.

JAPANESE IRISES

Once Iris laevigata was considered one of the parents of the gorgeous race of Japanese irises. Now the latter are believed to have been derived wholly from I. Kaempferi, and laevigata is found in our gardens only as a species, with one or two varietal forms. It is readily distinguished from Kaempferi because its leaves have no raised midrib and the standards are nearly as long as the falls. Though many beardless irises enjoy much moisture during their growing season, laevigata is one of the few true bog plants. It is happiest in a pool or where it is wet throughout the year, though it will grow in a border if constant attention is given to keeping it wet through the summer. I flowered it in Berkeley under these conditions last year. Its blossoms, borne in heads of three on stems eighteen inches or more high, are of as lovely a deep blue as can be found in the iris family. For the color alone it is worth cultivating. There is also a rare pure white form and a variety called albopurpurea, in which the white flowers have falls attractively spotted with blue. I have seen this variety flourishing where it was permanently planted in a small pool in a British Columbia garden.

The spectacular Japanese irises, single and double forms in great variety of color, were derived from Iris Kaempferi by years of persistent breeding and selection, mainly by Japanese specialists. It is hard to understand why the general gardner does not grow some of the Japanese irises where he has the proper conditions, as they would extend the iris season for another month into July and also give him unique garden effects and material for flower arrangement. Perhaps better understanding of their requirements will revive interest in them.

CULTURAL CONDITIONS

Japanese irises are decidedly water-loving plants, yet during their period of rest in winter they resent moisture. They are therefore not bog plants nor suited to permanent planting in ponds. They may be flowered there, however, by the method employed in San Francisco's Golden Gate Park, where they are grown in deep redwood boxes which are submerged during the growing season and removed in autumn to a dry situation. The Japanese grow them where they are flooded in spring and summer and drained in winter. In many places they will grow and flower happily under ordinary border conditions with due attention to thorough watering before blooming, if dry spells occur.

Their preference is for a rich lime-free soil containing plenty of humus and animal manure. They are heavy feeders and never successful in light hungry soils. Where neutral or acid soils are not found the use of aluminum sulphate to acidify the natural soil is recommended. A greater problem in many gardens is the high lime content of the water supply, which unless modified injures the plants. To combat this condition also, aluminum sulphate may be used.

As to the best time for planting, from July to September is widely recommended; in the colder parts of the country this allows plants to get well established before winter. Early spring planting is also practiced as it is easier to split up old clumps before leaf growth has begun. In warmer areas and those with dry summers, later fall or very early spring planting is better. Do not plant single shoots but good strong divisions of about half a dozen shoots spaced a couple of feet apart, the crowns about two inches below the surface. This assumes the planting is to remain undisturbed for three to five years. During that time, to insure large and plentiful bloom, it will be necessary to continue feeding by mulches of manure or applications of commercial fertilizer in early spring.

Japanese irises are easily raised from seed preferably sown in autumn in frames or pots. The seed germinates outdoors in early spring and a fair proportion of the little seedlings, if moved out into the garden and grown on strongly through the summer, will flower the next year. In view of the wide selection of fine named varieties it is questionable whether it is worth while raising seedlings, most of which will certainly be inferior.

SELECTION OF VARIETIES

The choice of varieties from catalogues is fraught with difficulties. Those raised in Japan, and many of the best have come from there, arrived here with their Japanese names. Because these are hard to remember, American importers and growers often translated the Japanese into English or gave them entirely new names. Some varieties were a good deal alike, which induced substitution, and the raising and naming of American seedlings further complicated the situation.

The first decision to make is whether you prefer singles or doubles; most of us grow both. The singles have the usual three short upright standards and three falls. These singles are natural and graceful in form. The so-called "doubles," which have been frequently described by those who do not care for them as resembling dinner plates, are large, generally flattish flowers in which the little standards have been converted into large petals similar to the falls. In some cases all six petals droop, in others they are ruffled, but the effect is flat. The doubles, with their ample petalage, are showier than the more graceful singles.

To help in choosing varieties I have made the following short list, arranged by color and divided into singles and doubles and including only outstanding varieties and those still offered by American growers. Longer lists are to be found in Mrs. Thomas Nesmith's paper, "Japanese Iris for Our Gardens" (Bulletin of the American Iris Society No. 80, January 1941), and in the fine chapter on Japanese Irises by Eleanor Westmeyer in "Garden Irises," American Iris Society St. Louis, 1959. This list reflects my own preference for solid as against complicated color patterns. Others might prefer some with more elaborate markings or even the mottled or striped varieties which are anathema to me.

Singles

    Butterfly Prince (Payne) pinkish with mulberry styles
    Hoyden (Marx) white falls, red-purple standards
    Miss Simplicity (Payne) white flaring
    Morning Mischief (Marx) sanded blue-violet
    Pillar of Fire (Payne) red with white veining
    Royal Sapphire (Payne) royal purple
    Royal Tiger (Payne) white ground with purple halo

Doubles

    Blue Lagoon (Marx) clear blue, early
    Fashion Classic (Payne) lavender
    Good Omen (Marx) deep wine velvet

Hisakata (Higo) deep blue violet
Ocean Mist (Marx) soft sky blue with deeper margins
Pink Frost (Marx) light pink ruffled
Pin Stripe (Marx) white, veined blue, with blue styles
Rose Tower (Marx) ruffled rose with white center
Sky and Water (Payne) ruffled medium blue-violet
Snowy Hills (Marx) snowy white, tall
Iso-No-Kamone (Higo) pure white ruffled

THE SPURIAS UNDER CULTURE

No one seems to know why one group of tall fine irises
have been called "spurias," which means bastards. Even in
these days of promiscuous use of the term there is no justi-
fication for its application to a true species and hybrids of
impeccable parentage. While within the group there is wide
variation in height, size, and color of bloom, all are characterized by strong upright growth, fine stiff swordlike foliage
persistent through much of the summer, and tall stems borne
well above the leafage with branches so short that the flowers
appear to be growing right out of the main stem, one above
the other. The species bearing the name Iris spuria which
we found widely scattered over southern Europe, varies in
height and size but always has blue flowers. It is now sur-
passed in size and beauty by the hybrids to which it has contributed. The species still worth growing are from Asia.

Iris ochroleuca, native to the wet lands in Asia Minor
which dry out completely in summer, is a tall strong species
with milky white flowers of somewhat spidery form not unlike those of the Dutch irises, with a yellow blotch of varying
size on the fall. Iris Monnieri is so similar to ochroleuca that
it is possibly not a distinct species but a pure yellow form of
the latter. Iris aurea, from Kashmir, is somewhat shorter, but
as it bears three or four clusters of golden yellow flowers

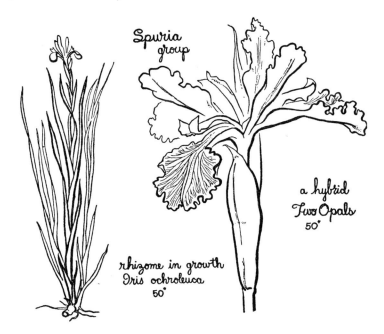

Spuria group

a hybrid
Two Opals
50°

rhizome in growth
Iris ochroleuca
50°

along its three- to four-foot stem it has a value of its own;
aurea is less vigorous, however, and much slower in settling
down to flower.

Spurias want to be planted in full sun. They have no special requirements as to soil and do well in whatever the average garden provides. They want plenty of water in spring
when making growth, but after flowering they go through
the rainless summers of California without watering, though
summer rains will not bother them. Because they do not
make their new root growth until early autumn and their
rhizomes do not retain their vitality well when out of the
ground, it is desirable in colder places to plant spuria irises
in September; in warmer sections planting can be done any

time in autumn. The rhizomes should be set just below the surface of the ground and to avoid frequent replanting it is best to place them as far as eighteen inches apart. When once established they may be left for years without division if occasionally fertilized. When good clumps have formed, they are most effective in the garden.

There are few geographical limits to the successful growing of the spurias. They have done very well as far north as Portland, Maine, with its cold winters, yet seem perfectly suited to Yuma, Arizona, which has a national reputation for summer heat. All along the Pacific Coast they grow like weeds.

Growing the spurias from seed is hardly worth while excepting for the breeder seeking to improve them by cross-fertilization and rigid selection of the best out of many seedlings. Seed should be sown half an inch to an inch deep in autumn; germination follows in spring, when the resultant seedlings should be moved out in rows to where they will flower, often the second year.

For garden use the spurias are most effective either in masses by themselves or in clumps of a single variety towards the back of the herbaceous border. With their fine foliage and tall stems, they are eminently suited to the latter location and have points of superiority over the tall bearded irises. The limitation has been in the range of their colors, but this is being considerably enlarged.

As cut flowers spurias have no equal in the iris family other than the Dutch irises, which they exceed in length of stem and size of flowers, so that there is little competition in their decorative use. They may be cut when the buds are showing color and because of the close placement of the flowers on the stems they are easily shipped; they are doubtless destined to become important florist flowers when the finer varieties, now expensive novelties, come down in price.

IMPROVED HYBRIDS

Over sixty years ago Sir Michael Foster raised improved forms of Iris ochroleuca, of which the best known is Shelford Chieftain. From crosses between Iris Monnieri and some forms of the blue spuria he got much taller, more vigorous blue hybrids like Lord Wolsley and A. J. Balfour. Much later, in Nashville, the late T. A. Washington raised and named a series of spuria hybrids mainly in blue shades which were great improvements.

In recent years activity in breeding spurias has centered in southern California, where the pioneer breeder, Eric Nies, established for himself an enviable reputation and introduced many new varieties. His Bronzspur was the first brownish spuria, and Blackpoint the first solid dark brown to be introduced.

The following recommendations are based on the opinions of others as well as my personal observation. For the beginner the older, less expensive varieties will give satisfaction. The connoisseur will want the novelties recommended.

White with Yellow Markings. I. ochroleuca or one of its improved forms like Shelford Giant (Foster) or White Heron (Milliken)

Yellow of Various Tones. I. Monnieri, Sunny Day (Sass), Wadi Zem Zem (Milliken), Investment (Craig) the last an indispensable novelty

Blue and Lavender. Harpeth Hills (Washington), Blue Rocket (Mrs. Washington), Dutch Defiance (Nies), Saugatuck (Nies), Azure Dawn (Nies), Morningtide (Walker) blue-white

Bronze and Brown. Fifth Symphony (Nies), deep yellow-veined brown, Monteagle (Washington), Russet Flame (Nies), Golden Agate (Nies), Bronzspur (Nies) and Blackpoint (Nies), newest brown

Blends and Bicolors. Pastoral (Nies), yellow and light blue, Lark Song (Nies), frilled white and yellow, Fairy Lantern (Nies) blue and yellow, Royal Toga (Nesmith) violet and white

THE WINTER-FLOWERING IRIS

Of the few remaining Old World beardless species I rate Iris unguicularis—unfortunately the botanists have decided that this jawbreaker rather than the easier I. stylosa is its right name—as by far the most important. I am at a loss to understand why any gardener, even if not an iris enthusiast, whose climate will permit him to grow it outdoors can bear to be without this iris. Even if I were again living on the Atlantic Coast I would find some way to grow unguicularis in a cold frame, in permanent pots or boxes in a warm window, or in a greenhouse.

The best and earliest forms are native to Algeria. Typically the flowers are rich lavender with white reticulations and yellow markings at the base of the falls. The size of the flowers varies considerably but in the best form they are from three to four inches across and both standards and falls are quite broad. There is a pure white form with a yellow signal on the fall; like many albinos, this is smaller and less vigorous. Recently a few iris specialists in the Pacific Northwest have been offering what is called a pink variety, really a very lovely and distinctly pinkish lavender. In our central California garden a good planting of these irises will produce flowers from October to March.

For garden effect it is desirable in September to cut back the evergreen foliage, as otherwise the flowers will be hidden among the leaves; they have no real stems but are held up on

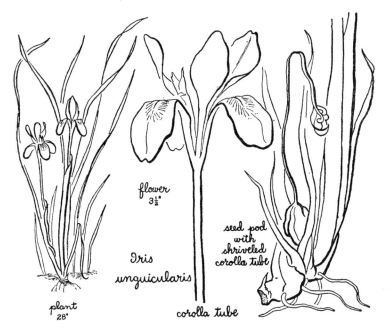

flower
3½"

Iris
unguicularis

seed pod
with
shriveled
corolla tube

plant
28"

corolla tube

perianth tubes from six to eight inches high. This iris is chiefly valued as a cut flower: a low bowl of it is a beautiful table decoration. In a recent severe California winter when all the usual outdoor flowers were frozen it was still possible to pick unguicularis in January and February. The flowers should be gathered in bud and gently removed from their base so as not to destroy other buds. They will open next day in water and although they may last only a couple of days more there are always others coming on to replace them. A later flowering variety with rich purple flowers blooms here in February and March but it is less valued than the early type. There are also Grecian and Cretan forms which are later and smaller.

In England unguicularis is always planted in a hot sunny situation as it enjoys summer baking. In comparable climates this would probably be the best situation, but in California where this iris is most grown it is quite as happy on the east side as on the west side of a wall. It does not want a rich soil; to give it this might result in too great a growth of foliage at the expense of flower. Any ordinary garden soil will suit it and I have never given mine any fertilizer whatever, nor does it ever get water except when it rains.

New plantings may be made either in April just after the season is over, or even better in September as the new root growth begins after the long summer rest. Divisions of the woody rootstock with several shoots should be planted at least a foot apart to allow room for spreading, as plants should be left for many years. Old crowded patches, unmoved for years, still flower well. While established plants are never watered, it is of course necessary to water new plantings until growth gets under way. For additional plantings or gifts I just remove pieces from the margins of the existing clumps without greatly disturbing these at all.

The adventurous can of course raise this iris from seed which matures below ground level as the ovary is at the base of the long perianth tube. This method of propagation, however, cannot be recommended for other than breeders working for new varieties.

Iris unguicularis should be tried outdoors in the southern states though it may not succeed under all conditions, particularly much summer moisture. Miss Caroline Dormon writes enthusiastically of her success with it in northern Louisiana. It should be tried in the semiarid southwestern states which have climates not unlike parts of southern California where it is successfully grown. It may be found in gardens the whole length of the Pacific Coast right up into British Columbia, where the temperature sometimes goes down close to zero. It has been grown in Washington, D. C., and even as far north as New Jersey in cold frames which not only keep the roots warmer but protect the flower buds as they develop.

THREE HARDY IMMIGRANTS

Iris Pseudacorus, common wild yellow flag found in marshes or even in water in central Europe, is an attractive species with rushlike foliage and stems three feet or more high carrying yellow flowers, the falls of which occasionally have central brown veining. It is best adapted to planting in or near water where it is so happy that it often naturalizes, but it is not dependent on such moist conditions and can be grown satisfactorily in an ordinary border. In California it flourishes at the edge of a lawn where through the rainless summers it still gets moisture from the sprinklers.

Iris foetidissima, another native of Europe including England, is a plant of little beauty in its flowers, which are of dull purplish gray and quite inconspicuous, though better yellow-colored forms exist. It is only grown for its bright scarlet seeds which are very ornamental and are sometimes seen in florists' shops. This is one of the few irises which thrive in much shade, though it flowers and therefore seeds less freely under such conditions. In the cool foggy summers of Berkeley it does not ripen its seeds; in the warmer, sunnier summers of Marin County, just across San Francisco Bay, it is reported to readily develop colorful seeds, which under most conditions are best cut for indoor decoration as they deteriorate quickly in the garden.

Iris dichotoma bears the common name of "vesper" iris as it opens in late afternoon and closes in early evening. The evanescent flowers varying in color from white to reddish purple are carried on a two-foot, much branched stalk. Its chief value is that it blooms in late July, August and early September. It is not an exciting species. Coming from Siberia and northern China, it is very hardy, but it tends to die out after flowering, possibly from exhaustion. It is easily raised from seed, which is the usual method of propagation, and early spring sown seedlings will often flower the same season. It likes a warm sunny position and is pretty indifferent as to soil, but wants water in midsummer before blooming.

CHAPTER SEVEN

History of Bearded Irises

The bearded irises comprise all those members of the family which have at the base of the drooping petals or falls a more or less conspicuous linear growth of short fuzzy hairs. Botanically they are referred to as the "pogon-irises" ("pogon" being the Greek word for beard). The latest classification is "eupogons" or true bearded irises, as compared with their nearest relatives, the oncocyclus and regelia irises. In nature they vary from minute plants with flowers only a couple of inches above ground to large vigorous species with strong broad leaves, carrying large flowers on branched stems up to four feet. For garden purposes they are divided into the miniature dwarfs, standard dwarfs, intermediates, table, border, and tall bearded irises. This chapter will deal chiefly with the remarkable development of the rather unexciting tall bearded irises of fifty years ago into the magnificent modern race of garden hybrids.

THE SMALLER BEARDED IRISES

In the mountains of southeastern Europe grows a very dwarf iris properly named Iris pumila. Some long-available forms and hybrids of this species are easy to recognize in gardens by their earliness, relatively slender growth, and almost stemless flowers carried on a perianth tube two to three inches long.

Dwarf Iris
Snow Maiden
12"

However, many dwarf bearded irises masquerading under
this name are really forms of Iris Chamaeiris. This very
variable plant, native to southeastern France and northwestern Italy, is characterized by foliage which is often persistent
in winter and by flowers with real stems. The garden varieties have stems up to eight or ten inches; colors include white,
yellow of various shades, pale and dark blues, and dark
purples. Though many named varieties were offered in English catalogues by the end of the nineteenth century, the first
serious attempt to improve and diversify these dwarfs was
made by W. J. Caparne about 1900. His charming introductions have not disappeared entirely from American and Eng-

lish catalogues. In the United States, Sam Burchfield some
thirty-five years ago in Michigan and later the H. P. and J.
Sass brothers in Nebraska introduced improved varieties
many of which are still listed.

For many years the dwarf bearded group was rather neglected. About ten years ago a revival in their growing and
breeding with a trend towards the development of smaller,
daintier flowers which could be regarded as miniatures rather
than dwarfs was led by Walter Welch of Indiana. He formed
the Dwarf Iris Society and drew in many people who were
interested in all aspects of dwarf breeding. Though as recently as 1954 most of the miniature dwarf bearded varieties
listed in catalogues had been introduced ten to twenty-five
years earlier, this breeding has been so fruitful that almost
all varieties now listed have been introduced since 1954.
They constitute a vastly superior race of little garden hybrids
suitable for rock gardens and edgings.

About fifteen years ago Paul Cook of Indiana crossed a tall
bearded iris with pollen from a true pumila and a new class
of middle-sized or median irises was born. Later, he sent
some pumila pollen to Geddes Douglas in Tennessee who
produced a whole series of these median hybrids which he
named "lilliputs." The amazing charm and vigor of the
Cook and Douglas hybrids set off a new wave of interest in
hybridizing an increasing number of dwarf bearded species,
and early in 1957 the Median Iris Society was formed. Since
then so many varying hybrids have appeared that all bearded
irises under twenty-eight inches have been reclassified. The
American Iris Society has now established five classes to replace the previous designations of "dwarf" and "intermediate."

The miniature dwarf bearded irises are species and garden varieties normally less than ten inches in height, generally unbranched, and with one or more terminal buds. They are usually the first to bloom in the spring, and are sponsored by the Dwarf Iris Society.

The standard dwarf bearded group is between ten and fifteen inches tall and includes all species and hybrids in this height range, including "lilliputs."

Typical
Intermediate Iris
Southland 14"

The intermediates are hybrids between dwarf and tall bearded irises which are between fifteen and twenty-eight inches in height and bloom just before the tall bearded. In colder climates where the tall bearded iris season comes in late May or June, the intermediates have had some value in filling in the gap following the dwarfs, although their color range has been quite limited.

Caparne worked for many years in improving the intermediate group, and at one time many of his introductions—some of them coming to us after naming by Goos & Koenemann—were listed and fairly widely grown. Later American breeders took up this line in a mild way, and William Mohr, Colonel Jesse C. Nicholls, and the Sass brothers introduced some valuable and distinct intermediates. Then came a decline in popularity, but the introduction of new blood, by such hybridizers as Wilma Greenlee and Clarence Jonas with resulting variation in color and superior form has revived interest in them.

The miniature tall or table irises, though of the same height range as the intermediates, are smaller and daintier with slender wiry stems, and they bloom at the same time as the tall bearded.

Border irises are shorter varieties of tall bearded and, of course, bloom at the same time. They may be anywhere from fifteen to twenty-eight inches in height. This class has long been needed: many charming varieties have been discarded because their height could not be stretched, even with imagination, to twenty-eight inches—the shortest a tall bearded iris can be.

TALL BEARDED IRISES OF THE OLD WORLD

Tall bearded irises, from some species of which our modern garden hybrids have been derived, grow wild only in Europe and Asia, more specifically from Austria through the Balkans and Asia Minor to Arabia. However, as the rhizomes will survive even though dry for months, some of the species and hybrids have been found over a far more extensive area, apparently carried by travelers or settlers. From its home in Arabia Iris albicans was carried along the whole northern coast of Africa, where it was planted in Mohammedan countries, and even into Spain when the Moors invaded that country. Centuries later it was brought over to Mexico and from there by the early settlers to California, where it is still the commonest iris. Often it is found apparently growing wild, but always near former habitations.

The so-called "Iris germanica" is certainly misnamed because it has never been found wild in Germany, though quite widely spread over southern Europe and western Asia. It is now generally accepted that germanica is not a true species, its varying forms being hybrids of unknown parentage. This is the very common blue and purple iris (a red-purple form is called Kochii), which is so widely found in America, particularly in the West. The old and formerly much grown I. florentina is merely an albino form of germanica. These irises, which are almost sterile plants, have not entered into the parentage of our modern garden hybrids. I wish to emphasize this because I have been told so frequently by unobservant iris growers that the fine varieties which they have purchased and planted in their gardens have reverted to the old purple or white. What unquestionably has happened in such cases is that in the ground where the new irises were planted there had at some time been plants of albicans or germanica and that when these were removed little nubbins had accidentally been left; being tough and vigorous, these eventually displaced the more delicate newcomers.

It is now accepted that all the tall bearded hybrids introduced before 1900 were derived from two European species.

One of these is Iris pallida, found in numerous forms from the south Tyrol down the Dalmatian coast. This iris is readily distinguished by its glaucous foliage, its short side branches, short perianth tube, and scarious or papery bud spathes; the flowers are of self colors in many shades of lavender and blue, even to purple. The form called plicata, with white ground and lavender or purple edging, has not been found wild but is botanically indistinguishable from Iris pallida and doubtless derives from it. The other parent of our older hybrids is Iris variegata, which extends south and east from Vienna through much of the Balkans. It has thinner, narrower, greener foliage and shorter stems, with two or three lateral heads of flowers; the yellow standards and yellow falls are so often variegated with chestnut or dark red that the general effect is of brown. Though extremely hardy, being accustomed to cold winters and summer moisture, it languishes and often dies out under arid conditions.

When I. pallida and I. variegata were grown together in gardens and the seed collected from them sown, a wide variation in color and pattern was the result. Even by the end of the sixteenth century there were many distinct varieties. When visiting the Prado in Madrid I came across a picture of a bunch of bearded irises by the Flemish painter Jan Brueghel, a son of the famous Peter Brueghel. Painted somewhere around 1610, these irises show a variety of colors and include one of the plicata pattern, which was apparently in Netherlands gardens as early as that time.

For the next couple of hundred years there was evidently no great change in the character of these earlier irises, but in the first half of the nineteenth century nurserymen began paying more attention to them, especially in France. In 1841

M. Lemon issued a catalogue in which he listed a hundred varieties with descriptions. Many of these were still among the standard commercial varieties offered by English and American specialists in the first decade of the twentieth century. Other continental raisers—Philippe Verdier, Louis Van Houtte and others—and in England John Salter and Peter Barr added to the number of these hybrids and to the confusion of the nomenclature by giving English names to continental, mainly French, introductions. About 1873 Barr issued a descriptive list of his extensive collection, arranging the varieties in groups: aphylla (including forms of germanica), amoena (white standards and purple falls), neglecta (lavender standards and dark falls), pallida (lavender, light and dark blue, and rosy-toned purplish selfs), squalens (forms with blended, often rather dull, combinations of smoky blue and gray or yellow and red), and variegata (clear yellow standards and falls either veined a dark red or of nearly solid ox-blood color). Barr's classification was adopted and continued in English and American lists into the nineteen-twenties. Even to this day such terms as "amoena" and "variegata" are applied to modern hybrids of these old color patterns.

THE BERTRAND FARR COLLECTION

In 1901 I began gathering together a collection of what few varieties I could find in Canadian and American nurseries and growing them in Montreal, my native city, but it was not until I imported a collection from Barr & Sons in 1905 that I felt justified in claiming to have the best then available. That same year Bertrand Farr, as I learned later, made even more extensive importations from this English firm. A few years afterwards, when he had established a nursery at Wyomissing, Pennsylvania, Farr issued the first of a series of beautiful catalogues which have become collectors' items. The varieties were arranged according to Barr's classification, well described, and featured in many cases in attractive color plates.

There is no doubt that the gathering together of this collection and its most attractive listing were primarily responsible for the interest in the tall bearded irises that developed in America in the first quarter of the present century. Moreover, Mr. Farr raised many beautiful and distinct seedlings, such as Juniata, Wyomissing, and Quaker Lady. In 1915 at the Panama-Pacific Exposition in San Francisco he had the most modern and comprehensive garden of the tall bearded irises, including not only the finest of the older varieties but some additional ones raised by Amos Perry in England, and a series of variegatas, amoenas, and squalens from Goos & Koenemann, the only German introductions of any importance.

This collection was acquired by Carl Purdy and remained in California. From it I added all the recent European and Farr introductions to my iris garden, for by this time I had moved to California and was living in Berkeley, just across the Bay from San Francisco.

OLDER DIPLOID HYBRIDS

Though the older irises lacked the opulence of the modern hybrids, being far inferior in size, form, and substance of flower, in brilliance of coloring, and in height and branching habit, they represented the culmination of the breeding possible from the combination of Iris pallida with I. variegata.

Like their parents they were what the geneticists call "diploids": that is, they had only two sets of twelve chromosomes, and were therefore limited in their development. Though not show flowers, as garden plants they were extremely effective. Each clump produced far more flower spikes than do the modern bearded irises, and though these were shorter (from eighteen inches to three feet high) and close branched, the mass effect of the thinner, narrower blossoms was even better than in the case of the larger, looser growing, shyer flowering moderns.

The older hybrids were particularly adapted to the scale of small gardens and they possessed hardiness, vigor, and a freedom from temperament not always found in the iris of today. Their toughness and persistence cannot fail to impress anyone driving along a New England road in early June, noting the casual conditions under which they have been growing for years in farm and cottage dooryards. I for one regret that they have almost wholly disappeared from the catalogues of iris specialists; the best of them—Pallida dalmatica, Juniata, and Albert Victor among the blues, Edouard Michel among the red-purples, Iris King or Fro in the variegatas, Rhein Nixe and Victorine among the amoenas, Jacquesiana, Nuée d'Orage, and Quaker Lady among the blended squalens, to name only a few—had places as garden flowers not readily filled by more recent introductions.

MODERN TETRAPLOID HYBRIDS

It is quite understandable that The Iris Society in England has established the Foster Memorial Plaque, awarded annually for distinguished service in iris culture, since Sir Michael Foster, Professor of Physiology at Cambridge Uni-

Diploid
and
Tetraploid
irises
compared

15"

an old diploid iris
small, narrow, thin and high branched

a modern tetraploid
iris with well
formed flowers nicely
placed on well branched
stem, Moongoddess 34"

versity, is certainly responsible for the development of the modern race. Growing and breeding irises as a hobby, he was instrumental in having collected in the Near East in the eighties and nineties certain wild irises which were the first "tetraploids": that is, they were tall bearded irises with four sets of chromosomes, plants of size and vigor, with tall branching stems and large flowers. Crossing one of these, Iris cypriana, with pallida, Sir Michael raised Caterina, Crusader, Lady Foster, and other hybrids. They also proved to be tetraploids, with tremendous potentialities for improvement in range and variety of color, substance, size, branching, and other qualities. Later in the hands of two American breeders Caterina became the ancestor of some of our best irises. From a cross which Foster believed to be I. pallida dalmatica by I. kashmeriana (a white collected on the Persian Gulf) he also raised two tetraploid white irises, Kashmir White and Miss Wilmott. The former became one of the progenitors of the large modern whites.

At the beginning of this century certain other Asiatic tetraploids came into the hands of the French firm of Vilmorin-Andrieux et Cie.; intercrossed or bred with diploids, these gave such remarkable advances as the tetraploid varieties Oriflamme and Alcazar, both important parents in later breeding. In southern France, Fernand Denis, an amateur, crossed the tetraploid I. Ricardii, sent him from Palestine, with some of the older bearded irises and raised a wonderful series mainly of tetraploid hybrids, such as Mme. Durrand. These were imported into California by Mrs. Jeannette Dean about 1918. The Denis hybrids, however, lacked adaptability to rigorous climates and excepting for Mme. Durrand, which is the parent of Jean Cayeux, the strain was not much used.

Some of the hybrids raised by Vilmorin and by Denis were "triploids"; that is, they had three sets of chromosomes or a total of thirty-six, rather than the four sets of the tetraploids, giving forty-eight. Loute, Isoline, Mlle. Schwartz and Leverrier were all triploids; this largely nullified their value in breeding, as irises with this chromosome count rarely bear fertile seed.

Later than any of these, during World War I, A. J. Bliss, an English breeder, raised the famous Dominion by crossing the diploid Cordelia and the blue-purple Armenian Iris amas. The new tetraploid was of such heavy substance that the falls were held almost horizontally; they had great depth of color and a rich velvet texture. From this parent he later raised Cardinal, Bruno, Grace Sturtevant, and other varieties with the same characteristics of substance and velvety falls, but with longer stems and more vigorous habit. Fernand Cayeux, in France, used Bruno in producing the many rich flowers which were sent from France to America in the late twenties and thirties; and in the United States many breeders used Cardinal in the development of better red irises and Bruno to improve the variegatas.

AMERICAN BREEDERS

In America the pioneer breeders in the development of the modern hybrids were Grace Sturtevant, William Mohr, and the Sass brothers. In her Wellesley Farms garden Miss Sturtevant raised many beautiful diploid irises, in particular Shekinah, the best yellow in its day and later an important parent in breeding. Her work which has contributed most to the development of the modern race, however, was the crossing of Mrs. George Darwin, a small and only slightly marked plicata, with Foster's Caterina. The resulting tetraploid hybrid of great vigor she named Sherbet, and this with its derivatives, Rose Madder and others, did much to improve reds and variegatas.

In the perspective of thirty-five years it is now possible to rate William Mohr the outstanding American breeder. Through his work with Iris mesopotamica and Foster's Kashmir White, American breeders were given in the late twenties such outstanding irises as Conquistador, bred from the diploid Juniata by the huge ungainly mesopotamica; El Capitan, bred from Oriflamme by mesopotamica; Purissima, which came from a seedling of Caterina by Kashmir White crossed with Conquistador; the epoch-making tetraploid plicatas, San Francisco and Los Angeles, and many others. After his tragic death in 1923 all his seedlings came into my possession, and most of those introduced were my selections. These introductions formed the basis for breeding by all the earlier California breeders, Dr. Stillman Berry, Professor E. O. Essig, Carl Salbach, and myself. Mohr had been particularly anxious to raise large deep yellow irises, but it took years of work on my part and the introduction of Dominion and Alcazar blood before I succeeded in getting the series of yellows, outstanding in their time, Alta California, California Gold, Happy Days, Naranja, and Fair Elaine among them.

The importance of the work of the Sass brothers was at first in the production of irises which could stand the rigors of their Nebraska home. Later the Sasses pioneered in the production of large yellow-ground plicatas, of blends such as Prairie Sunset, of whites and white-ground plicatas like Blue Shimmer, and in their latest work of yellows, culminating in Ola Kala.

A quite different phase of American iris breeding has followed these pioneers. Hundreds of introductions, nearly all tetraploids and many of outstanding quality, have found their way into iris catalogues and innumerable breeders, mainly amateurs, have joined in the exciting game of trying to raise irises of improved form or color. In some cases this has been achieved merely by the selection and mating of two named varieties and in this way most amateurs begin; but in due time to get distinction the breeder develops a line of seedlings of his own with the characteristics he values most. These he intercrosses, only occasionally bringing in new blood from varieties he did not raise. In this way Dr. R. E. Kleinsorge in Oregon has developed his fine line of large, colorful, shapely blends; Mrs. C. G. Whiting in Iowa achieved her attractive coppery and nearly orange introductions; David Hall in Illinois, after getting certain early breaks, perfected his line of tangerine-bearded pinks; Dr. Robert J. Graves in New Hampshire bred his wonderful blues and whites; Paul Cook in Indiana has achieved his magnificent deep blacks and unusual amoenas; and such breeders as Tell Muhlstein in Utah and the Schreiners in Oregon are developing the newly popular crinkled and laced-edged varieties.

CHAPTER EIGHT

Bearded Irises — Culture, Propagation, Diseases

The bearded irises have an enviable reputation for ease of culture and longevity. This is doubtless due to the presence of clumps of very hardy diploids in old gardens east of the Alleghenies and particularly in regions of continuous winter snow. These were the only varieties up to twenty-five years ago, their variegata and pallida parentage adapting them to climates of cold winters and summers with quite occasional rains. In coastal California the tall bearded irises are of equally tough character. The old ones, Iris albicans and florentina, and the newer ones bred from the tetraploid cypriana and mesopotamica are both perfectly adapted to a semiarid climate quite similar to that of their countries of origin around the eastern Mediterranean.

The modern hybrids, bred between the diploid and tetraploid races, naturally vary considerably in their adaptability to the various climates of the United States and Canada. Although the tendency is to develop varieties which will do well right across the continent, some of the earlier hybrids like Purissima soon die out or stop flowering in very cold or wet climates and those with a dominance of variegata or amoena in their make-up are unsuited to the dry summers of the Southwest or of California.

There are considerable areas to which the tall bearded

irises do not adapt well: the largest one in the United States is the coastal plain of the lower South, say from Charleston, South Carolina, along the Atlantic and the Gulf of Mexico as far as eastern Texas, where they are shy bloomers. Varieties derived from species of eastern Mediterranean countries are successful as far south as Baton Rouge, Louisiana, and Houston, Texas. The other area to which they are less suited, though the hardier varieties can be grown there, takes in the northern tier of states from the Great Lakes to the Rocky Mountains and the adjacent provinces of Canada. I have sent many irises to friends and relatives in Winnipeg, and though some varieties do fairly well for a while, many of them show a distressing tendency to die out in spite of greater care and protection than they get elsewhere. In the heavy clay soils of Saskatchewan they are still less successful. The solution here may be in the breeding of varieties suited to local conditions.

DRAINAGE AND SUN

Wherever they are grown it must be remembered that these irises are not water-loving plants, that in nature they are to be found only where drainage is good. This matter of drainage is the most important consideration in their garden culture. Where the bearded irises are planted on hillsides, slopes, or in soil which has fine natural drainage there is no particular problem. On the level and especially in heavy soils raised beds are generally necessary to insure that water does not lie on plants during wet seasons; otherwise there will be danger of too much sappy leaf growth and too little bloom and of bacterial soft rot during warm weather.

The tall bearded irises also demand a sunny position. This

does not mean that everywhere they must have full sun all day, but if much of the day is spent in shade they will produce their fans of leaves with few or no flowers. Too much shade in my experience is by far the commonest reason why there are complaints about failure to flower. As to aspect, there seems to be no special preference: on the eastern side of a hill they are likely to be later and to last longer in flower, while on the western side they come into bloom earlier, the season tends to become shorter, and the individual flowers are less lasting.

SOIL AND FERTILIZERS

For many years writers always recommended for irises a soil on the alkaline side and where this did not exist suggested the incorporation of lime or broken plaster as a corrective. Unquestionably irises are being grown in many places on soils which contain considerable lime, but it is now generally accepted that they are happier in a neutral soil or one slightly acid. This accords completely with my own experience, for I have had no difficulty whatever in an untreated neutral soil.

In most climates a rather light soil is preferred, though it should be one which contains considerable humus. Very light sandy soils such as one finds along the coast need the addition of humus and heavier materials to give them more body and they will require more fertilizing than soils of medium weight. Heavy soils, particularly with poor drainage, are a liability where there is a high rainfall, but where the summers are dry, irises can be grown very successfully even in the heavy black adobe of the valleys.

It has been my experience that fresh soil which has not previously been used for growing irises will produce fine plants and flowers for some years without fertilization. As time goes on if the same space must be kept in irises, the ground must be fertilized. It is desirable to replace several inches of soil by new top soil with plenty of humus in it. This reconditioning is important for continued success. The bearded irises are not very deep rooters; nevertheless, digging the ground to a depth of at least a foot will promote a much better root growth; digging even deeper would be better.

Almost everyone writing on fertilizers for tall bearded irises used to warn against the use of animal manure, but opinion has completely changed in recent years. An early experience of my own caused me to question the advice against using manure. When I was gathering together a collection of irises in Montreal I happened to see several clumps of what appeared to be wonderfully improved varieties in the garden of a florist at the entrance to Côte des Neiges Cemetery. Naturally I wanted to acquire them, but the honest nurseryman told me that they were just ordinary varieties making marvelous growth because he had dug holes a couple of feet deep and put a wheelbarrow of horse manure in each before replacing the soil and planting several rhizomes of a variety to form eventual clumps.

It is still good practice not to endanger the rhizomes by using even thoroughly decomposed manures for surface dressing or forking into the upper six inches of the soil. Incorporated in the ground well below the rhizomes where the feeding roots can get it, it is now generally believed to be safe. Irises are now known to be heavy feeders and too much nitrogen supplied in any form tends to promote luscious foliage at the expense of flower spikes.

In the preparation of poor soil plowing or deep digging and the incorporation of animal manure or garden compost is essential. I prefer to use the compost because I can make it near at hand. If manure is not available use Driconure, Bovung or other commercial dried manures. Wood ashes (which have not been rained on) are a valuable source of potash. Fortunately, readily available commercial fertilizers are quite satisfactory and good results are usual if bone meal is mixed in with the soil at the time of planting so that a good deal of it is down where the roots can readily get it, or hoed lightly into the surface later. Most growers stick to inorganic fertilizers, with a preference for bone meal, but a good many for upkeep rake in Vigoro or some comparable complete fertilizer, and the practice of using superphosphate in this way is increasing.

WHEN TO WATER AND PLANT

If the soil is dry when planting is being done, it should either be watered ahead of time so as to be pleasantly damp or the beds should be given a good watering to settle in the irises after planting. After resetting plants it is undesirable to continue heavy waterings until it is quite evident that root systems have been established capable of making use of the moisture. Bacterial soft rot can readily follow excess watering of plants still almost dormant. In climates of summer rains the tall bearded irises get quite sufficient moisture naturally, sometimes too much, but in those parts of the continent which have no summer rain it is desirable to give these irises an occasional thorough soaking. Once a month

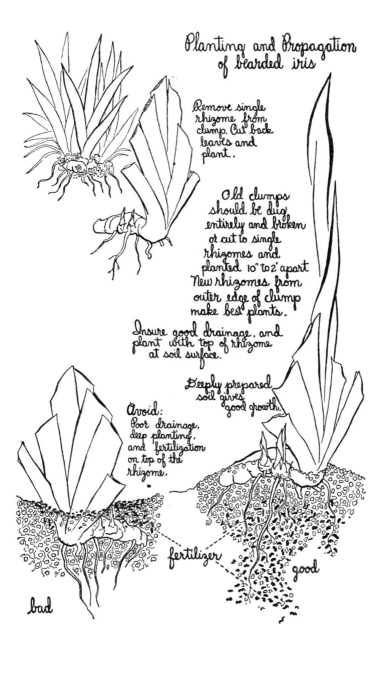

Planting and Propagation of bearded iris

Remove single rhizome from clump. Cut back leaves and plant.

Old clumps should be dug entirely and broken or cut to single rhizomes and planted 10" to 2' apart New rhizomes from outer edge of clump make best plants.

Insure good drainage, and plant with top of rhizome at soil surface.

Deeply prepared soil gives good growth.

Avoid:
Poor drainage, deep planting, and fertilization on top of the rhizome.

fertilizer

good

bad

would be often enough to do this. Even in semiarid California, in gardens in the cool, foggy coastal belt, established plantings are quite capable of going through the rainless summer without irrigation.

The best time (not necessarily the only time) to plant irises varies quite considerably in our numerous American climates. Shortly after flowering, the tall bearded irises begin the development of a new root system, as can easily be seen by the examination of a rhizome in late June or early July. This is the easiest time to divide and replant irises because there is no mass of fibrous roots to spread out. If the rhizomes are planted just beneath the surface they will soon develop these fibrous roots and establish themselves thereby. Late June or early July is the preferred time in the colder climates of eastern Canada and the United States and in the prairie country, but even there we have the alternative of planting early enough in fall so that the irises are established before cold weather.

The advantage claimed for early fall planting is that between July and late August the embryo flower buds have been developed in the rhizomes and there is greater certainty of bloom next season. Where the plants have been disturbed earlier, they may devote themselves to leaf rather than bud production. In the South, even as far west as Texas, where summer rains are often excessive for unestablished plants, fall planting after the really hot weather is over is generally preferred. On the Pacific Coast and particularly in California practice varies a great deal. Growers in the north, where there are occasional summer rains, lean toward late June and early July planting. Further south some prefer late May and early June planting, which necessitates watering and weeding through the long succeeding dry summer, while others defer most of their planting until September or October or even later in the year, as there is no danger of heaving by frost.

The most widely accepted present practice is to plant the rhizome with the top just covered with soil. Some claim better success by leaving the top of the rhizome exposed, and still others believe in covering the rhizome with an inch of soil. It is a matter very largely to be decided by conditions of drainage, summer rain, and the amount of sunshine available to ripen the rhizomes, which in nature go quite dry in summer. Where planting is done after the fibrous root system has been developed, as will be the case in late summer and autumn, the roots should be spread out with an inclination downward before firming in. It is desirable to cut tops back to six or eight inches; retaining too much leafage causes excessive evaporation and in a windy area makes it difficult for the plant to remain firm in the soil. Besides, extra leafage is untidy and unnecessary.

The distance apart needs some consideration. Good husky iris rhizomes, if left unmoved for three years will cover so much ground that it is advisable to plant them no closer than one foot apart. This will avoid too much replanting. Where several rhizomes are being planted to form a clump of, say, three rows in depth, the separate rhizomes may be alternated in the rows and there is much to be said for planting them all in the same direction, as the increase is never backward, but forward and from the sides. Where the planting is on a slope it is advisable to put in the rhizomes with the growing end headed upward. However, when clumps of varying size are being arranged in a border, there is some advantage in an arrangement which will provide the growth be in all directions away from the center of the clump. This device makes it possible two or three years later, when the clumps have even grown into each other, to determine which plants belong to each variety.

LABELING

One of the trials of collectors is the problem of labeling; cheap labels are impermanent and permanent ones are expensive. We have found no better device than galvanized wire stakes, the top being bent around into an overlapping circle. There are some relatively inexpensive embossing machines with which the name or number of the variety can be printed on metal strips. Punched and attached to the stakes by copper wire, these give a permanent inscription although it cannot easily be read at a distance. Plastic strips and labels are now available. A cheaper alternative is to use wooden white-painted labels, writing in India ink. These again should have copper wire, never steel which disintegrates in a year. Such labels may last a season or two and are legible at some distance, but the quality seems universally poor and they need constant replacement. We have learned that no matter how well plantings are labeled it is wise to make plans of all beds, writing in the names of the varieties and the number of rhizomes at time of planting. With this in hand, not only can we replace lost labels but we are often able to identify varieties in bloom without the necessity of stepping onto broad beds.

WHEN TO REPLANT

Perhaps the commonest question asked is how often the plants of the tall bearded irises need division and resetting.

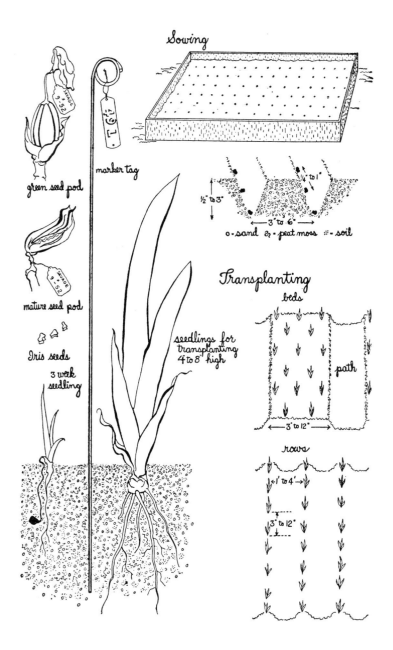

On the average a newly planted bed is at its best in its second and third years. Thereafter it tends to get crowded and have an undue proportion of the ground occupied by old, no longer flowering rhizomes. As the rate of increase varies with the vigor of particular varieties and with culture, it is unwise to be dogmatic. It is always possible to delay the replanting of whole beds by chiseling off the back rhizomes which have become woody and without growth and then filling in the holes with good soil mixed with some inorganic fertilizer.

When replanting is necessary, the clumps should be dug up and all soil removed by shaking or washing; then the still actively growing rhizomes which will be on the circumference of the clumps may be removed and used for the new planting. Sometimes double rhizomes are used and enough is left to provide nubbins or buds along the side, the balance being simply discarded. When it is desired to increase stock rapidly, such older rhizomes as show signs of growth along the sides may be planted separately as single rhizomes or they may be cut before planting into pieces with single buds. The former method is easier. The nearly dormant buds thus separated from the active growth at the ends will soon turn green and send up leaves which will develop into fans. Though they do not bloom the succeeding year, thereafter they are quite as good as any other rhizome. Commercially much propagation is done by this supplementary method.

Most growers of bearded irises do not provide winter protection. The plants seem quite able to take care of themselves on the Pacific Coast, in the South, and in the southern half of the Middle West. In New England, the states around the Great Lakes, and in the Northwest, where winters are very cold, growers cover varieties which by reputation or experience are considered at all tender. Salt hay, excelsior, straw, cornstalks, and leaves are among the materials used, sometimes less to keep out the cold than to prevent heaving due to alternate freezing and thawing.

DISEASES AND PESTS—BACTERIAL SOFT ROT

When growing a large collection of bearded irises in eastern Canada many years ago, I noticed that while they were flowering in mid-June in what was unusually warm humid weather, some of the flower stalks were falling over and some of the leaves turning yellow. On examination I found that both the stalks and the leaves were rotting off and that the rhizomes to which they were attached were already soft and mushy, with an unpleasant odor. This was my first experience with bacterial soft rot. I had the disease identified as a bacterial one favored by heat and moisture. As a period of very dry sunny weather followed, the rot made no further progress and the affected rhizomes eventually recovered.

Bacterial soft rot is a serious disease of irises and fairly widespread, though relatively little known in California where the dry climate of late spring and summer does not favor it. Treatment consists of removing all rotting stems and leaves and cutting out of affected rhizomes all diseased tissue until one gets to that which is clean, white, and solid. The rhizomes which are left in the ground should be soaked with a rose-red solution of potassium permanganate. It is generally unnecessary to lift the affected plants. If any are so badly diseased as to justify lifting they should be soaked for a short time in the potassium permanganate solution and left for a few days to dry in the sun before replanting. Soft rot may be in part due to poor drainage, planting too deep, over-watering when not fully established, warm and wet weather conditions in early summer, or to bacterial infection following borer injury, though rot does not always follow borers. No specific preventives are known but good cultural practices, including full sun, avoidance of manure as a top dressing, a regular program for borer control and in case of infestation the above-described treatment, will arrest the disease before plants are killed, though some bloom may be lost that particular year.

WINTER ROT

Another form of rot, called botrytis rot or winter rot, in which the rhizome is covered with a feltlike fungous growth, is troublesome in some sections. Sometimes little or no spring growth occurs, and the plant dies. Breeders in the Northwest and Idaho are recommending the use of fungicides such as Captan either to dust the rhizomes before planting or as a drench which may easily be applied with a sprinkling can after a thorough cleaning up of the beds and the cutting away of all diseased rhizomes.

CROWN ROT

Sclerotium or crown rot is caused by the mustard seed fungus. It attacks the bases of the leaves, and other rot organisms may enter the rhizome through the diseased tissue. Moisture, shade and warmth favor its development; sunshine, air circulation and good drainage are its enemies. It is a serious disease only in very wet periods. Dr. A. W. Dimock of Cornell University in an article on Pests and Diseases in the

AIS Bulletin 154, part 2, July 1959, recommends the use of a new fungicide, Terraclor, as a drench for plant and surrounding soil. One level tablespoon per gallon of water is the correct dilution. This serves both as a preventive and a control.

LEAF SPOT

Sometimes in its early spring growth (not uncommon in coastal California) and sometimes after flowering (more common elsewhere) the broad leafage of the bearded irises is disfigured by a fungus, Didymellina macrospora. It does not kill the plants, though it may be debilitating, and some varieties are apparently more subject to it than others.

Professor A. E. Waller of Ohio State University recommends a two-year program for the elimination of leaf spot. Start in late autumn by removing all dead and infected leaves on and around the iris beds and burn these, as they contain the spores responsible for the leaf spot. As some spores will have escaped to the soil around the plant clumps, both soil and plants should be sprayed or dusted, according to current recommendations, with the fungicide zineb. Begin as soon as new growth starts in the spring, and continue at weekly intervals as long as the leaves are in active growth. DDT, for the control of borers, may be mixed with this material, which goes under such trade names as Parzate, DuPont Fungicide, etc. The DuPont and Ortho vegetable dusts also contain zineb. A bacterial leaf spot, or leaf blight, is appearing here and there among iris plantings, in appearance similar to the usual leaf spot, but more destructive to the leaf tissues. This disease, too, is encouraged by wet, humid weather. No control is known. Infected leaves should be cut off and burned.

SCORCH OR FIRE AND PINEAPPLING

Occasionally the leaves of an iris plant will turn brown as though scorched. On examination the rhizome will be found to have turned red and the fibrous roots to have died. Little is known of the cause of this disease, which has been variously ascribed to excessive drought or to the lack of some chemical elements in the soil. Scorch has been reported checked by thoroughly soaking the soil with water to the depth of a foot and twelve hours later disinfecting it with copper ether control, Lawna-gen, a tablespoon to a gallon of water, by sprinkling the solution on the soil at the rate of a gallon to ten square feet. Success has also been reported from soaking the affected plants in a solution of potassium permanganate and replanting in fresh ground after a period of a couple of weeks during which they have been allowed to dry out. Generally small nubbins will soon appear along the sides of the rhizomes and they will regain the roots which were completely lost during the attack of the scorch.

A mysterious disease to which the name of "pineappling" has been given has recently been noticed, particularly in southern California. It is characterized by all the growths throwing up abortive flower stalks with no new leaf or root growth. I have had it once or twice from plants newly brought into my garden, and though it has generally meant the loss of that plant the trouble has not spread to any adjacent ones. No cure or preventive has yet been discovered.

IRIS BORER

The iris borer has been a serious problem in certain parts

of the eastern United States with the heaviest infestation around Washington, D. C., and in Pennsylvania. In the Far West it seems to be quite unknown, certainly I have never seen borers in California or heard of any infestation on the Pacific Coast. Generally about the time the irises are blooming the worm can be spotted traveling down inside the central leaf, and by squeezing the leaf it may be eliminated. If not discovered then, it will work its way down into the rhizome from which it will have to be dug out with a knife. Constant vigilance is necessary for control by this primitive method, and iris growers have therefore sought practical preventive measures.

Experiments with DDT have given excellent results in killing the newly hatched borer between leaving the egg and getting to the iris leaf. As the hatching of the eggs is intermittent and extends over about two months from the opening of spring, weekly applications to the plants and the surrounding soil and shrubbery for a distance of twenty feet from the irises are necessary. A dust under the name of Protexall was tried in one garden very successfully, this being a combination of DDT, Rotenone, sulphur, and Fermate. Another method suggested for either dusting or spraying is a combination of DDT, malathion and zineb.

Dusting is the easiest method; it should be done early in the morning on windless days using 5% or 10% DDT dust. For spraying the recommended formula is: per gallon of water, 2 tablespoons fifty per cent DDT Wettable, one level teaspoon Du Pont's Spreader Sticker and zineb, according to directions on the package. The DDT is added to a tank of water and thoroughly mixed, and then the Spreader Sticker is sprinkled on it and mixed in. As this is not a solution but a suspension it has to be frequently shaken or stirred up to maintain a mixture.

In view of the rapid increase of effective preventives and controls for plant diseases and pests, growers are advised to consult the Bulletins of the American Iris Society for latest developments.

It will be noted that clean culture, drainage and sunshine are stressed as control measures for each disease. Clean, well-fed (but not overfed) irises are more resistant to disease than the same varieties crowded into weedy beds.

CHAPTER NINE

Bearded Irises—Breeding and Raising from Seed

The only way to perpetuate or increase the number of plants of any particular tall bearded iris is by division of the rhizomes. These garden-bred plants are of such complex heritage that even if self-fertilized they will not come true from seed. The objectives of breeding are to achieve advances in any desired direction: flowers of better substance and form, with taller, better branched stems; new colors or improve those we have, as in working for purer blues and deeper yellows. Plants are also bred for greater vigor or adaptability to the climate in which the breeder is working. Examples of the last are the use of Purissima, an unsatisfactory plant in cold climates, as the seed parent of pure whites which are perfectly hardy in Illinois or New Hampshire, or the attempts of California breeders to raise variegatas adapted to rainless summers.

The tall bearded iris has become what it is today largely through the work of amateurs who made most of the early pioneer crosses of value and who continue to produce in their gardens a large proportion of the fine new irises eventually distributed through commercial dealers. Hundreds of American and Canadian amateurs are now raising annually thousands of seedlings, possibly between a quarter and a half million. From these their raisers will optimistically select, name, and register several hundred; most of those registered will never be introduced into commerce, and of the two or three hundred which eventually will appear in iris catalogues, it is unlikely that more than one in ten will be found listed after five years. This statement is made, not to discourage the amateur breeder, but to indicate the terrific competition which any new variety must face today, even to survive in commercial lists for a decade or so before being superseded.

In the American Iris Society's Official Symposium of 1948 of the hundred favorite irises of today, only four, Wabash, Great Lakes, Sable and Snow Flurry, had been introduced more than twenty years ago, and only eight other varieties were introduced before 1947. The chances, therefore, of the average amateur's making money from the sale of outstanding seedlings are very slight. He should enter into this exhilarating adventure for other reasons. Most of us get very real satisfaction from raising something of our own, selecting from a lot of seedlings just those which happen to appeal to us. In the present situation it is also relatively easy to raise batches of seedlings of such high quality that many may be selected for one's own garden. A cross, for example, of Snow Flurry by Chivalry, which flowered with me last year, gave so many lovely blues of different shades that it was hard to select from them. Again, the crossing of a couple of the new tangerine-bearded pinks will certainly give the amateur a lot of attractive pink flowers for his own garden. The pleasure which comes from watching the first flowering of a batch of seedlings of one's own will be his at little cost.

STRUCTURE OF THE IRIS FLOWER

The iris, like most of our garden flowers, has both the
female and the male organs of reproduction in each blossom.
If pollen is placed on its stigma it is then being used as the

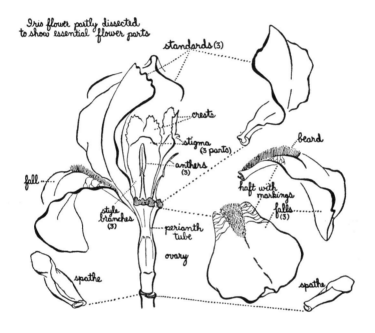

Iris flower partly dissected
to show essential flower parts

standards (3)

crests

stigma (3 parts)

anthers (3)

beard

fall

haft with markings

falls (3)

style branches (3)

perianth tube

ovary

spathe

spathe

female or "seed" parent, but if its pollen is placed on the
stigma of another variety, then the same flower is being used
as the male or "pollen" parent. An examination of the
flower shows that it has three upper petals or standards, three
drooping petals or falls. From the center of the flower extend three style branches, each finishing in a sort of crest
below which will be seen a little shelf, the stigma or recepta-
cle for the pollen. Underneath each style branch there is a

single anther, which as the flower fully opens develops the pollen or male element. Just beneath the flower where it is joined to the stem will be found a rounded enlargement which is the unfertilized ovary and eventually becomes the seed pod. At the base of each fall is the haft, and on this grows the linear collection of hairs known as the beard. Beginners sometimes think that this has something to do with the reproductive process. It is true that in the flower as found in nature bees may be attracted by the beard, crawl into the center of the flower for nectar, and in backing out carry with them pollen which is accidentally deposited on the stigma of another iris. Possibly because of changes in the garden flower bumblebees no longer find this an entrance, for iris flowers appear rarely to be accidentally crossed by insects in the garden. The beard is no more essential than has been the comparable ornamentation of the human animal. Without either, life goes on.

HOW TO CROSS-BREED

Take a pair of what are known as eyebrow tweezers—fingers are a bit clumsy; remove an anther from the flower selected as the male or pollen parent and, holding it by the tweezers, gently scrape off the pollen onto the stigma of the plant selected as female or seed parent. That is really all there is to it. Arguments have arisen as to whether, for complete fertilization, it was sufficient to apply pollen to one of the three stigmas or necessary to pollinate all three. Many breeders continue to use the latter process from habit or feel that it improves the chances of fertilization, but there is no question now that the walls of the ovary are permeable and that it is possible to fill the three chambers, with their double rows of seed, from a single pollination of one stigma. Many breeders do not bother to remove the anthers from the flower to be used as seed parent; others believe that they reduce the slight chances of self-pollination by removing all anthers when making the cross. This is absolutely necessary in beardless species, which are subject to self-pollination at an early stage of development of the flower. Still more careful breeders cut off the falls so as to leave no landing field for flying insects, but few if any cover the flowers with cellophane bags as is done in strictly scientific experiments. Conditions being good and the varieties compatible, there will develop from the pollen, tubes running down into the ovary, through which the pollen will reach and fertilize the seeds.

HOW TO STORE POLLEN

It is often desired to use the pollen of an early flowering variety on one which does not open until later in the season. Various methods are used to keep the pollen dry, which is essential to its viability. Some breeders put anthers into small gelatin capsules such as are now universally used to facilitate taking medicine; others use tightly sealed cellophane envelopes. In either case the containers should be kept in a refrigerator or other cool dry place.

Many of us use a homemade desiccator. You can easily make one from a large broad-mouthed glass jar on the bottom of which is placed a half inch of calcium chloride, readily obtainable at the drugstore. Cover this with a piece of cardboard or two or three layers of paper. If the weather is at all damp when pollen is gathered, it should first be dried, though I have found it generally satisfactory to put the anthers directly into small paper or cellophane envelopes on which is written the name of the variety and the date of pollen collecting. These envelopes can be grouped as is most convenient, by color or whatever will facilitate the work of the breeder. I, for example, keep all tangerine-pink pollen envelopes together with an elastic band, plicata pollens, and others divided into groups. These envelopes are placed unsealed in the desiccator, which when not in use should be kept in a cool place with the top tightly screwed on. I have found that pollen so stored will keep the full length of a California six-weeks iris season and have sometimes sent it to friends with even later seasons. It is in fact quite possible to send properly dried pollen by air mail to England and still have it viable on receipt, though in this case the pollen envelope should be sealed before mailing. Desiccator-stored pollen falls off onto the envelope, from which I scrape it with the tweezers and put it on the desired stigma. Many breeders prefer however in such a situation to use a small camel's-hair brush. This method involves having a good many brushes or sterilizing them by dipping them in alcohol after each use, a procedure I find too much trouble.

In some cases it will be found that the variety completely lacks pollen; Purissima is an outstanding example. It can, however, still be used as a seed parent and has been widely employed for such purpose. Some few varieties seem incapable of setting seed, but may have perfectly good pollen, so that their characteristics may be transmitted through using them as male parents. Occasionally a variety will turn up which has no pollen and will not set seed, and is therefore the end of its line.

Stigmas of iris flowers are generally receptive soon after the flower fully opens and remain so until shortly before it collapses. How soon the stigma is receptive is shown by the development of a certain stickiness of its surface. Fertilization is far more likely when a period of clear dry sunny weather follows the crossing. On the Pacific Coast there are periods of low wet fog during the iris season when it is difficult to get "takes," presumably because the atmospheric conditions are unfavorable to retaining the pollen dry until it has penetrated the ovary. Experiments in covering the flower with cellophane to keep out excessive moisture have turned out well.

HOW TO KEEP RECORDS

Some of our earlier breeders achieved excellent results without keeping records of the crosses they made and sometimes even used mixed pollen. Today even the amateur breeder believes he will get greater satisfaction and be able to work more systematically if he keeps accurate records of what he does. When making crosses the simplest procedure is probably to use the thin cardboard price tags obtainable at all stationers'. Even the smaller sizes have room to write the abbreviated name of the seed parent followed by a cross and the name of the pollen parent: Snow Flurry $\times$ Chivalry. Where unnamed seedlings are being used a number must be substituted for one or both of these: Loomis VQ72 $\times$ 6-18-1, the seed parent in this case being an unintroduced tangerine-bearded seedling raised by Dr. Loomis, the pollen parent a 1946 seedling of my own. These labels should be looped over the perianth tube below the flower when the cross is made; after the seed pod has formed, the label should be moved down to the base of the seed pod so that it will not be lost. I have found that these labels last until the seed is ripe, but where climatic conditions or wasps gathering paper for their nests disfigure the labels, it is wise at the end of the crossing season to go over the labels for all the crosses which have set and paint the record with shellac. Some breeders keep a record of crosses as they are made, especially where they have in mind to try certain combinations, possibly planned during the winter months in lively anticipation of the season to follow.

RIPENING OF SEED AND SOWING

The process of seed ripening is often quite slow, taking two to three months depending on climatic conditions. Where tall stems have several pods it is worth while staking these to avoid accident during that time. If the stem should be broken by accident after the green pod has reached its maximum size, it is possible to ripen the seed by standing the stem in a sunny place in a bottle, with or without water. Water is probably desirable only where summers are quite warm and dry. The seed pods may be harvested as soon as they turn yellow or brown and begin to open at the top; if they are left longer the seed is apt to scatter. It is my practice to remove the beautiful amber-colored seeds from the pods while they are still plump and smooth, shelling each pod into a small bag or envelope on which I write the parentage found on the label. These envelopes I keep in a dry sunny place until I am ready to sow the seed. If some of the lots get mildewed I simply rub the seeds in my hands, which seems to remove the mildew and provide an oiled surface against later mildewing. I have no evidence that mildew has ever affected germination.

There has been much controversy as to the relative merits

of sowing the seed as fast as it ripens or allowing it to dry and become hard and wrinkled. Though reports show earlier, in fact some fall, germination from fresh seed sown at once, this may be a doubtful advantage excepting in climates with no real winter. Apparently a large proportion of early germinating seedlings fail to survive cold winters and those that do show little advance in growth over the seedlings from early spring germination. The practice in sowing seed must depend largely on the quantities to be taken care of. If there are not many lots and these contain relatively few seeds there is no reason why pots should not be used, one for each cross. Wooden boxes not less than five inches in depth will do, or in California and comparable climates the plebeian tin can may be substituted. Cans have the advantage in dry climates that the soil does not dry out so quickly as in clay pots.

For large lots of seed it is necessary to prepare special seed beds. On perfectly level ground where there is no danger of soil washing or animal molestation, beds are often made right in the open ground and are quite successful in my own experience where the natural soil is light and friable. On slopes or where moles or gophers are prevalent, or where the natural soil is rather heavy, there are real advantages in making permanent beds which can be cleaned out every second year. The soil can be replaced and beds used again. Mine are constructed of one-inch redwood boards, eight to ten inches wide, and I have found that a frame three feet wide by twelve long makes a desirable unit. After the ground has been leveled and the boards nailed together, a bottom of half-inch galvanized wire cloth is attached to allow contact with the moisture below the bed and keep out rodents. Fill up the bed to within an inch or so of the surface with a light soil mixture containing a good deal of sand; this makes germination and weeding easier. Level off and water thoroughly to settle the soil, and when it is dried out enough sow the seeds about an inch deep and about an inch apart in single or multiple lines across the bed, leaving at least an inch between one lot of seed and the next.

For labels I have used strips of zinc cut from one half to an inch wide and about six inches long. This gives enough length for them to hold well in the soil leaving plenty of room at the top to write the number of the cross in India ink, which I find quite permanent. The zinc strips can be used again and again by removing the old writing with sandpaper.

It is also possible under favorable conditions to sow the seeds at least two or three inches apart in the open ground, leaving all the seedlings to flower just where they germinate. This is tough treatment but is probably still resorted to by some breeders who work on a very large scale. It is not good practice for the amateur, however, as the seedlings naturally are pretty badly crowded when they bloom and the selection of the best is therefore difficult.

GERMINATION

The germination of iris seed is slow; it often remains dormant for one or more seasons. In cold climates seed collected late the previous summer and sown in October will begin to germinate in April and May. In warmer climates where the seed is ripened earlier, though sown at the same time, it will begin in February and be nearly through for that spring by April. Seed from some crosses will germinate very well the season after sowing—I have found that seed from Purissima, Snow Flurry, and other Purissima derivatives comes up well the first year; other seed parents—Orchid Lady is a good example—rarely give much germination the first year, but after a year of dormancy there is pretty good germination. It is therefore highly desirable to retain one's seed bed or seed containers for at least a second year, after which, though there will continue to be sporadic germination, it is probably not worth while retaining any but rare and valued seed.

In experiments in Berkeley extending over several years, Professor E. O. Essig of the University of California reported a total of thirty-nine per cent germination from beds kept two years. At Cornell University, Professor L. F. Randolph reported thirty-five per cent first-year germination during a period of four years. Sowing the seeds under greenhouse conditions failed to shorten the period of dormancy or increase the percentage of germination. Therefore if cold frames are used it should be merely for preventing heaving, because winter cold to freezing point or lower seems to promote germination. It has been my experience in Central California that germination is much better after cold wet winters than after warm dry "tourist" winters, and when dry spells occur in January or February I flood my seed beds. Professor Randolph improved germination somewhat by chipping the seed and submitting it to near freezing temperatures and by leaching it in running water, but Professor Essig found germination not improved by chipping, prechilling, or planting seeds direct from the pods before drying. For seeds which are particularly difficult to germinate, and this includes oncopogon crosses, where the experience is that they may lie dormant for years, the really persistent breeder will find it worth while to read the material on "Embryo Seed Culture" by Dr. L. F. Randolph in "Garden Irises," American Iris Society, St. Louis, 1959, where the very successful method of growing the excised embryo in sterile nutrient agar is described.

THE CLUFF METHOD

A neighbor of mine, W. B. Cluff, an amateur experimenter, has worked out the following simplified procedure for germinating difficult seeds or those reputed to be very delayed in starting growth:

Disinfect the dry ripened seeds in Clorox, but do not leave them covered too long as Clorox burns; about a minute is enough. Wash them off at once under the tap. Then put seeds in a glass saucer called an "agardish" and soak in water for about three or four hours. With fingernail take off helium end of seed—the small end where the embryo is found. Then soak again. Six hours later take a razor blade cut to hoe shape, screw a watchmaker's glass on your eyeglasses—it magnifies five times—lay a cardboard on the table and on it snip off the end of the seed so as to expose the germ. When cut, drop the seeds into a saucer with a little water to clean them.

For sterilizing use one crushed tablet of chlorazene (Abbott) in one fluid ounce of water. Into an agardish put two pieces of paper toweling cut to fit. Pour the agar solution in, leaving it about ten minutes. (This solution is made from Dehydrated Orchid Agar supplied by the Difco Laboratories, Inc., of Detroit, Michigan. Use very little, a quarter of a teaspoon to one and a half drinking glasses of water, letting this boil in a glass saucepan until the agar dissolves leaving a clear liquid. The solution is not stable, lasting only about four days, so make a fresh lot when it begins to coagulate.) Agar solution has all the food elements to make the germ grow. Put the seeds with exposed embryos on top of the aforementioned double layer of paper; on them place two more layers of the paper toweling; then add water and about six medicine droppersful of the agar solution. Let stand about five minutes, then drain off *all* the liquid with the medicine dropper. The paper is then supersaturated but not sitting in water. Cover the dish. Every day add water and solution, and drain it off for from five to seven days, which is all the time that is needed.

When seeds germinate, take them out. Use six-inch clay pots for sowing. Fill with very light soil baked in an oven at two hundred and fifty degrees for two hours. Fill pots to within an inch of the top, lay the germinated seeds on the soil surface and cover them with half an inch of the baked sterilized soil. Water with a fine spray until thoroughly wet, and with the dropper put some more of the agar solution on top of the soil. Cover the pot with Celloglass to hold moisture and keep out dirt. All will be up in about ten days, if the plants are coming at all. For damping off use a four per cent Clorox solution.

Cluff gets about two-thirds of the seed having embryos to grow in this way. He has no artificial heat, does the job in a washroom on the east side of the house which gets only fifteen minutes of sun a day, temperature at highest 65 degrees Fahrenheit, lowest 40. He believes a sunnier room would give stronger plants, but considers the important thing is to drain the glass so that water is not above the seed at any time.

CARE OF SEEDLINGS

After germination in the ordinary seed bed or container the only care necessary is to see that the young plants are weeded and given plenty of water. If they show any tendency to damp off in warm muggy weather the use of Fermate or a comparable fungicide is recommended and has proved effective in stopping it in my experienre. When the seedlings are two to three inches high with several roots, they should be lifted from the seed beds and planted out where they are to flower. If the beds are to be retained for a second year, this is best done by thoroughly watering them and just as the soil is drying out gently lifting the seedlings by inserting a handfork beneath them. I have successfully transplanted seedlings up to six inches in height, but it is difficult to get up all the roots when they are so large and the moving produces some setback, though the seedlings move better when too large than too small. While some growers like to plant out seedlings in lines, others prefer a four-foot wide bed with the seedlings about eight inches apart across the beds and the rows about the same distance apart. This is the method I now prefer, as it masses together the seedlings from a single cross, uses less ground, and is easy for weeding purposes.

The proportion of bloom the following year will depend upon the excellence of the culture and will vary greatly under different conditions. On level ground, where the summers are warm and either by rain or irrigation ample moisture is provided from the time the seedlings are set out until September, seventy-five per cent or more may be expected to flower the season after transplanting. Seedlings will take far more water than established plantings.

When flowering occurs some growers pull out immediately those plants they do not propose to keep; others, more conservative or perhaps concerned with the appearance of the seedling patch, prefer to stake those which they are going to keep and to describe or evaluate them by label, discarding all other plants which have bloomed when the season is over. In any case if seedling growing can be relegated to some inconspicuous part of the garden or even done outside on a nearby lot, the general garden effect will suffer less. Selected seedlings should be lined out by themselves for further trial, though the outstanding ones might well be divided at once to provide the maximum of increase. In later flowerings a large proportion of the original selections will be discarded as the breeder gains knowledge of irises and his standards become higher.

For most beginners, raising one's own must be the sole reward, but occasionally even an inexperienced breeder will get an outstanding seedling. Miss Ruth Rees, the San Jose schoolteacher who raised Snow Flurry, had one of the exhilarating examples of beginner's luck. Her procedure in selling the whole stock to a commercial grower who could introduce it properly suggests what might be done under similar circumstances, though many amateur breeders of national reputation prefer to sell their novelties themselves through their own select lists or to have them handled by a commercial dealer on a percentage basis.

CHOICE OF PARENTS FOR BREEDING

The genetics of the modern race of tetraploid tall bearded irises is highly complicated and still full of unanswered questions. The amateur breeder, hardly yet prepared for this study, may be comforted by the assurance that, though the breeders who have developed this race and those who are still making advances have worked carefully and thoughtfully and kept records of their crosses, they are not themselves geneticists and still work largely on the old trial-and-error method. Unquestionably the beginner will profit much by studying the parentages of the best modern varieties. These can generally be traced through the registration pages in the American Iris Society Bulletin. It will also help him to know that certain colors or patterns are recessive: to get these traits the parents on both sides must contain the recessive color or pattern sought.

WHITES

Pure white is recessive in the old diploid whites and in a few modern tetraploid whites, but in the great majority of varieties, derived largely from Kashmir White, it is dominant. White can be obtained by crossing one white with another or by crossing a white with other colors, generally blue. From Snow Flurry ✕ Katherine Fay (two whites) came New Snow; from New Snow ✕ the light blue Cahokia came the white Cliffs of Dover; and from Purissima ✕ the pale blue Cloud Castle was raised the lovely white Lady Boscawen. This same cross gave an even more distinguished pale blue sister, Helen McGregor, which, crossed with Cahokia, gave both recessive white seedlings and Blue Bird Blue. When the recessive white character occurs in tetraploid whites, it is usually in connection with the dominant character. The lovely recessive white Senorita Ilsa comes from the two blues Helen McGregor and Sylvia Murray, both of which, interestingly enough, have diploids in their pedigrees. A different kind of recessive white character from plicatas is found in a few white varieties such as Jake and Snow Velvet.

In the breeding of blues the outstanding variety Great Lakes has been the most potent pollen parent in recent years. It is found in the parentage of Chivalry, one of the best blues we have, which in turn produced the highly praised Sierra Skies and the 1958 Dykes Medalist, Blue Sapphire. There is considerable evidence that the clarity of the blues is improved by the inclusion of pure whites in the breeding. Cahokia and Pierre Menard, two outstanding new blues, have nothing in their parentage but Purissima, Santa Barbara, and Santa Clara, the last-named a derivative of Santa Barbara, which was bred from Kashmir White.

PLICATAS AND PINKS

The plicata pattern is also recessive, so to get new plicatas we must cross one plicata with another or a plicata by a seedling of plicata parentage. Theoretically it is also possible to get plicatas from two non-plicatas of plicata parentage, but as the occurrence of the recessive under these conditions in tetraploids is relatively rare (about one to thirty-five, not the old Mendelian ratio of the diploids), this is a slow and uncertain adventure. The beginner will find it easiest to assemble the best of the modern plicatas and intercross among them. Though plicatas are not now particularly popular, they do offer greater chances of variation and of new and interesting color patterns and combinations than do selfs. Having raised about ten thousand plicata seedlings since 1940, I can prophesy great fun for the breeder who wants to play with plicatas without consideration of profit.

The tangerine-bearded pinks have developed during the

past ten years from relatively small, short-stemmed flowers into varieties which have most of the fine qualities already achieved in whites, blues, or yellows. The tangerine beard is generally, but not inevitably, accompanied by a pure but pale pink flower. Cold deep lilac-pink colors, red-purples, even occasionally blues, crop up among the progeny of pinks in which the inhibitor of blue color is absent.

The tangerine beard is again a recessive. In a planned breeding of at least two generations the forward-looking breeder may outcross to obtain larger size, taller stem, or whatever else he desires. But he cannot expect the recessive coloring in the first generation unless by accident or design the flower he uses for the outcross carries the gene for the tangerine beard. This is true of the yellow Golden Eagle, for instance, and Midwest Gem. In any case his quickest way to get a lot of tangerine-bearded pinks is to cross a couple of the best existing ones, preferably of different parentage. For example May Hall, David Hall's fine achievement from his own strain of seedlings, could be crossed with Helen Louise (Lapham) which was raised from his two tangerine pinks of wholly different parentages, Barbara Luddy by Paradise Pink. Other parents of proven merit are Happy Birthday and Palomino (D. Hall) and Muhlstein's Party Dress and Pink Fulfillment. Important parents for the new tangerine-bearded whites, as well as for pink breeding, are Wallace's Cathedral Bells and Fay's Mary Randall and Native Dancer, the pollen parent of Plough's Cloud Dancer, a tangerine-bearded white. Lipstick (Fay) and Frost and Flame (D. Hall) are first developments in this breeding.

Since the 1930's, when I raised Alta California, California Gold, Happy Days, Naranja, Fair Elaine and other yellows,

I have not worked on the improvement of this color range, though other breeders still use these and Ola Kala which produced Randolph's fine new yellow Morning Sunlight. It is surprising that so little work is being done in the production of deep yellows. However, from a garden standpoint the need of more pale and medium yellows is even more important and the best of the lighter shades should be selected for parents for them. Some of the new light yellows such as the fine greenish yellow variety Limelight come from pink breeding.

A number of hybridizers are now working for a green iris. From Green Pastures, the first variety to show definite chartreuse color, has come Woodland Sprite (Copedge) which is said to be one of the best "greens" yet achieved. Green Fashion (Fass) is another advance toward green.

REDS AND BLENDS

The so-called reds, most of which are on the blue rather than the orange side, have been considerably improved as to fineness of finish and the elimination of heavy haft venation. As compared with the blues, whites, and yellows I have found that reds lack size and vigor and I know that many breeders are outcrossing such reds as the older Garden Glory to achieve these qualities. This is slow, difficult breeding; its many problems offer a great challenge to hybridizers, who are using brighter reds such as Defiance (Tompkins) and Queeche (Knowlton), brown reds like Bang (Craig) and Trim (McKee), coppery Tall Chief (DeForest), and the black-red Sable Night (Cook) in this work. So many warm blends have been raised in recent years that it is hard to improve them. Some have not proved as good growers in certain areas as in their originators' gardens and others have lacked stature.

Here there is real opportunity to blend the best of Dr. Klein-sorge's wonderful introductions such as Cascade Splendor and Chamois with the best blended colors from such breeders as Carl Salbach, Mrs. Whiting, and Fred DeForest. The great value of Tobacco Road in transmitting good form and substance to the flowers of its progeny has been demonstrated.

VARIEGATAS AND AMOENAS

In the variegata pattern, with its yellow standards and red falls, there are already many good modern examples, from the old City of Lincoln, to Mary Vernon, Staten Island, Gayhead, and Paul Cook's blue-falled variegata, Pretender. Here the achievement of broader petals and taller growth are desired, particularly in California, where variegatas tend to be shorter than elsewhere. The use of the broad-petaled Mexico will certainly assist in improving the form of the flower, but outbreeding with taller wide-branched seedlings or varieties is necessary to get height and branching.

Among the amoenas, flowers with white standards and blue- or red-purple falls, Wabash, an introduction of the middle 1930s, was long the outstanding variety though not a good doer in semiarid climates. Recently Geddes Douglas of Tennessee has been highly successful in this breeding. His near-amoena, the cream and red-purple Extravaganza produced two superior amoenas, Gaylord and Criterion. And from Criterion has come Bright Hour.

Today the definition of "amoena" is being expanded to include various colors. We have pink-falled amoenas (Baby's Bonnet, Baker '57), light blue amoenas (Whole Cloth, from Paul Cook's famous Progenitor line), and, of course, Mrs. Stevens' famous yellow amoenas, Pinnacle and Mystic Melody. Fair Elaine, known to possess the dominant inhibitor of anthocyanin, is in the parentage of the latter and of Marion Walker's new Channel Island.

THE SMALLER IRISES

For those interested in serious breeding of the smaller bearded irises, I recommend membership in the Median Iris Society, the Dwarf Iris Society, or both, though the independent hybridizer can produce many attractive seedlings by crossing his tall bearded varieties with pumilas to produce lilliputs, lilliputs with pumilas and pumilas with each other for miniature dwarfs, and tall bearded with lilliputs for intermediates. (The pollen from the early-blooming pumilas is stored as described on page 133 until the later varieties bloom.) A color assortment of pumilas, as White Mite, Red Amethyst, the blue April Morn, yellow Carpathia and deep violet Sulina, together with a few lilliput varieties, as Green Spot, Baria and Tinkerbell, with whatever tall bearded varieties the hybridizer already grows, are sufficient material for endless combinations. Color inheritances in this breeding are somewhat different from those in the tall bearded; interesting results may be obtained by crossing different colored varieties. The seedlings from all these crosses are usually vigorous, and frequently bloom their first year. This characteristic alone is enough to recommend the hybridizing of small irises to the backyard breeder.

THE ADVANCED BREEDER

The fun of iris breeding as well as the chances of getting something really distinct are greatly improved when the breeder has developed an individual line of seedlings of his own and does nearly all his breeding with them, only out-crossing to secure qualities not evident in his strain. It was when they reached this stage that Dr. Kleinsorge with his beautiful blends, Dr. Graves with his fine whites and pale blues, David Hall with his tangerine-bearded pinks, and Clarence White and Stafford Jory in their quite distinct lines of oncopogon breeding gave us the great advances for which they are so distinguished.

For the advanced breeder or the individual of scientific mind who wishes to know what has thus far been found out about iris genetics, I recommend the following two papers: the chapter on Iris Genetics by Dr. L. F. Randolph, and the long chapter on Breeding Bearded Irises, in the new "Garden Irises," a comprehensive treatise by leading iris specialists in America and Great Britain, published by the American Iris Society in St. Louis, 1959.

CHAPTER TEN

Planning the Garden with Bearded Irises

While the tall bearded irises overshadow in garden use the earlier miniature dwarfs and various medians, these little irises being both low growing and different in season have an important place in the garden scheme. I believe that the preoccupation of most gardeners and nearly all breeders with the tall bearded irises has reached its peak and that a return to much greater use of low-growing irises and interest in their improvement by breeding has already begun. Years ago I grew the latter in great variety in eastern Canada and later in California, and found them wholly satisfactory for the early spring garden on both coasts. Now after years of neglect, for which I owe them my apologies, I have acquired a collection of the best varieties of today. These I am trying out in a single patch, so that by a study of their size, height, and color as well as the sequence of bloom I may use them to the best advantage.

It must be realized that there is great variation between the tiny pumilas and their hybrids, and the larger series which have come primarily from chamæiris, and, of late, from many dwarf species crossed with tall bearded varieties. The newer arenaria hybrids, for instance, may best be grouped rather than interplanted with such larger-flowered and vigorous hybrids as Tinkerbell, Pogo, Lilli-White or Cloud Fluff.

WHERE TO USE THE SHORTER IRISES

The true pumilas and perhaps the dainty arenaria hybrids may appropriately be planted in well-drained pockets in a small rock garden, while the vigor, size, and mass of color obtainable from some of the larger varieties fit them better for drifts in a large rock garden. Many of us with hillside gardens have used rock walls for terracing; the tops of these walls afford particularly happy situations for the dwarfs because such situations bring them nearer eye level and culturally provide fine drainage. Though neglected for years and undivided, every spring a little patch of Iris lutescens, variety Statellæ, continues to flower here at the top of a rock wall to remind us of what we have lost by not using more of these little irises in this way. I have also found them quite easily cultivated on short steep slopes where their mass of little rhizomes creates a soil binder.

In informal gardens the miniature dwarfs are best used in drifts or patches, where their great profusion of simultaneous bloom gives delightful color almost on the ground. They may be combined successfully with the earlier spring-flowering bulbs and dwarf perennials, though these must never overrun or shade their rhizomes. Still another use of these dwarfs is as groups, edging plants along the front of a herbaceous or mixed border, where they may be combined happily with early perennials of very different leafage and effect, such as Arabis albida, aubrietias, Alyssum saxatile, Phlox subulata, violas, or thymes. The standard dwarfs which are ten to fifteen inches tall combine charmingly with daffodils and early tulips, phlox divaricata, anchusa, doronicum and bleeding heart, and carry the season on to meet the Darwin tulips, the intermediate irises and even the early tall bearded irises. Though they can be used with discretion for edging the mixed border, I do not think that the use of little irises along the margins of beds of later blooming tall bearded irises is to be recommended, as bringing down the same leafage right to the path gives a monotonous effect. In garden arrangement, cultural problems necessarily arise; dwarf irises increase rapidly and ask for replanting every three or four years. After the first year they will appreciate a surface feeding of a little bone meal or other commercial fertilizer. They must be given plenty of sun to flourish.

From a garden standpoint intermediates are characterized by stems from fifteen to twenty-eight inches high which make nice clumps but not show flowers. Their importance is diminished by the still limited color range; there are whites, blues, yellows, and purples, and even one or two tangerine-bearded pinks, but in general the existing colors lack the brilliance of the taller hybrids. Their greatest value is in giving color to the mixed border in May and in flowering at the same time with the brilliancy of the tulips, to which the softer tints of the intermediates are often a good foil. They do not fit well into a garden devoted wholly to irises, nor are they particularly effective in masses by themselves. They are certainly most appreciated in colder climates where the tall bearded irises do not come until late May or June.

The border irises are the smaller talls, less than twenty-eight inches in height. For the windswept central states and today's many smaller gardens, these are more suitable than very tall varieties. The slender and dainty table irises, with the same height limits, are ideal for arrangements, or as delicate accents in the perennial border.

TALL BEARDED SPECIES FOR ACCENT

Among hardy plants for garden decoration in a great variety of uses—as specimen plants, clumps in the herbaceous border, massed in special borders or in segregated gardens devoted wholly to them—the tall bearded irises have no equal. They glorify early summer gardens wherever they are grown. They may have even a purely utilitarian value where as in southern France they are used to bind the soil on the face of steep terraces. When used for that purpose in a garden, however, it will be desirable to plant only very vigorous varieties of relatively low stature, not the long-stemmed hybrids of the modern race.

In any garden, but particularly in a small one where only a few irises are grown, specimen or sometimes small group plantings can be most effective among shrubs or herbaceous plants or in relation to an architectural feature—a bench, a pergola, or some location where the striking characteristics of the iris in bloom can be displayed. Here especially will be the place for a few plants of one of the magnificent white irises which because they are generally rather early or because white much used in a border gives a spotty effect, are best grown by themselves. This is how to use Purissima, which is not only tall and very early but so much an individual that it hardly fits into miscellaneous plantings. In California where it was bred, Purissima grows with the greatest ease and always flowers freely, but its very precocity has greatly limited its use in regions where late spring frosts too often maim the early foliage or blight the buds. Fortunately it has now many descendants which have varied its fine qualities without the tendency to winter growth. Among these are Snow Flurry, with its beautifully frilled flowers, New Snow, Lady Boscawen, and the more recent Cliffs of Dover, all hardy and vigorous wherever tall bearded irises are grown.

Sometimes these single pictures are best composed of a group of two or three irises of varying heights flowering at the same time, with a foreground of a low perennial whose color will repeat or enhance in value that of the irises. For example, a group might be made of the beautiful blue Chivalry with a pale yellow like Amadine and the low pure white Priscilla, with forget-me-nots and white arabis in the foreground. The gardener with a desire and the means to use the latest novelties could substitute the glorious light blue Sierra Skies and the pale yellow Butterhorn or Largesse, again using Priscilla, for which there is still no substitute among novelties. A striking combination could be made with the dark purple Violet Symphony and one of the deep yellows such as Solid Gold or Ola Kala, among the older varieties, or Gay Spring or Golden Hawk among the newer yellows.

Individual groups, particularly if they are to be viewed at close range, might be made in some cases of irises which blend less easily into larger plantings. The new coppery blends and the yellows and reds which follow the old variegata pattern could be cited. A group, for example, of Cascade Splendor with the lower Pretty Quadroon or Thotmes III to the front and a cream like Ruffled Organdy or Starshine for contrast would be pleasing. The nearly pure-white plicata Snow Crystal could be combined beautifully with the tangerine-bearded pink Helen Louise and a clear, pure, low-growing blue like St. Osyth in front. The patterned plicatas, usually difficult to place, are worth trying in groups with self-colored irises of the ground color of the plicata: for example, a pure white planted with the white-ground, blue-edged Blue Shimmer, or a tall yellow self with the low-growing, red-edged, yellow-ground plicata Ruth Pollock, and Alyssum saxatile citrinum and Arabis albida in the foreground. Restraint should be used in the number of such isolated little compositions; otherwise they may give a restless and spotty effect to the garden.

IN THE HARDY HERBACEOUS BORDER

A popular and practical use of a considerable number of tall bearded irises is in interval plantings throughout the hardy herbaceous border. If the border is shallow and short it will hardly be desirable to use more than one series of small clumps, preferably in varieties of medium height; put them in the middle ranks, the size of the clumps and their distance apart depending on the scale of the border. Proportion must be kept continually in mind, for if large clumps are put in a small border they dominate it, and small clumps in a long deep border would look lost. Consequently no definite number of plants can be specified for clumps; they might range from three of a variety in a small border to seven or nine in a very large one. In general the larger clump will look better if lengthened rather than increased in depth. A three- to five-plant clump would not have more than two ranks in planting, preferably arranged alternately, while a clump made up of a dozen plants should not be deeper than three ranks. Later in the season it is easier to mask out iris plantings which have length rather than depth.

BORDER OF PERENNIALS AND IRIS FOR EARLY SUMMER

Provision has been made for 10 clumps of tall bearded iris, 2 Spurias, and 2 Siberian varieties,

When the herbaceous border is sufficiently deep, say nine to ten feet, there will be plenty of room for two series of clumps throughout the border's length—a shorter clump two to three feet back from the path, a taller one at the five- to six-foot depth—so arranged that they alternate as viewed from the path, never in front of each other. They may even be so arranged that those in the rear rank are earlier varieties than those in the front rank, which will of course prolong the season but never give quite the luxuriant effect of plantings where all the varieties bloom at about the same time. This arrangement may seem to some gardeners rather stiff and formal. They are, of course, perfectly free to plan more casual and apparently less studied arrangements. The one proposed, however, has two recommendations: it does not mass the irises in any one part of the border, which they would overwhelm in their season and leave pretty uninteresting out of it, and it does provide a kind of rhythm throughout the length of the border. After all, the tall bearded irises are not modest plants which blend casually into any and all plantings; they have an assertive accent to their character and are fitted to tie together the less formal arrangements of associated plants. Garden plantings should not attempt to vie with nature, and the tall bearded irises are peculiarly unfitted for naturalistic planting. A hardy border should have some design in it and these irises greatly assist in establishing the pattern.

Irises planted in the herbaceous border should be selected for their color value in clumps rather than for the form and finish of the individual variety. It follows that standard varieties at hand in a complete range of iris colors and often at a mere fraction of the cost of scarce novelties will answer the purpose of effective planting. Sometimes the standard varieties serve even better than the novelties, which have still to survive the test of time and to justify themselves under the casual conditions of a mixed border. It is always wise to limit the varieties chosen for border use to those of clear clean color, in the main selfs, though in the forward line near the path an occasional bicolor, soft blend, or even plicata may be planted where study shows that these will enhance the color value of adjacent clumps. This, however, should be done with restraint.

I am sure that many artists and specialists in color arrangement will agree with me in advising against the promiscuous use of white as a peacemaker between varieties of natural discord such as strong yellows and russet blends. With the excellent moderate-priced creams and pale yellows now available, it is much better to use these, as they do not focus attention on themselves or give the spotty effect of glistening white. A simple way to arrange a sequence of clumps through a long border is to follow a scheme starting with pale pinks and whites, passing on to stronger blues and purples, followed by reds, paler blues and grays, with yellows in the distance; but unless irises are planted first and the rest of the border filled in later the associated plants will naturally affect the scheme. Much has been written about the various hardy herbaceous plants which can be appropriately associated with the tall bearded irises. If the border is expected to be attractive throughout the garden year it may be well during the season of irises to let them dominate, the other plants serving as foreground or background and offering no real competition.

There are certain hardy perennials, the long-spurred

columbines for example, which are lovely with irises because of the light and airy character of their flowers and the possible color harmonies or contrasts. Again, such perennials as the blue flax, Linum perenne in cold climates and L. narbonnense where winters are not severe, or clumps of pyrethrum in separate colors, by their lower growth and flatter form of flower offer no competition for attention and blend well into compositions. Along the path, too, it is possible in iris time to have clumps of a variety of marginal perennials, some of which will pick up the colors of the irises. This would leave large areas of the border for later summer- and autumn-flowering plants—hemerocallis, phlox, Michaelmas daisies and chrysanthemums, to mention just a few. But if the border is only intended to be effective in early summer, then it is possible to use with the irises, as is done in England and would be feasible in the Pacific Northwest and in some other favored areas, the perennial lupines of the polyphyllus type, of which the Russell strain is a popular one. The oriental poppies may also be associated with irises when they are in flower, though it would be a daring gardener who would attempt to use anything but the soft pink or lavender shades; the solid crimsons and the orange-scarlets which prevail in this family are best planted by themselves where they will receive the attention their colors insistently demand.

In planting irises in borders keep in mind not to plant near them other things which will shut off sunlight or when the irises have bloomed, shade the ground where they are growing and prevent the rhizomes from getting the sun and warmth necessary to their good health and future flowering.

BORDER OF TALL BEARDED IRIS

CAROLINE JANE — blue and white plicata	SOLID GOLD — deep yellow	ROSE GARLAND — light rose	FRANCES CRAIG — greyed lavender	SABLE NIGHT — red black	LADY ILSE — light blue	ELMOHR — red purple	SNOW CRYSTAL — white marked blue	BLACK HILLS — blue black	PIERRE MENARD — medium blue
BELLERIVE — cream	SARAH GOODLOE — maroon red	EXTRAVAGANZA — cream and purple	BIG GAME — violet blue	GOLDEN FLAME — rose red	LAVANESQUE — lavender	CHIVALRY — medium blue	PALOMINO — pinkish buff	HELEN McGREGOR — pale blue	HAPPY BIRTHDAY — light pink
CORDOVAN — red brown	SUNSET GLOW — copper blend	DARK CONTINENT — plum and copper blend	CLIFFS OF DOVER — warm white	HELEN LOUISE — deep pink	BLUE SAPPHIRE — pale silvery blue	MARY RANDALL — bengal rose	STARSHINE — cream white and faint blue blend	LIMELIGHT — lime yellow	CINNAMON TOAST — brown plicata
LEADING LADY — yellow and white	BLACK FOREST — black blue	BLUEBIRD BLUE — medium blue	ARGUS PHEASANT — golden brown	PATRICIAN — white marked yellow	LADY MOHR — lavender and beige	WHITE SPRITE — white white	VIOLET HARMONY — light violet	MIDNIGHT BLUE — deep blue	APRICOT GLORY — orange pink
CHANTILLY — orchid pink	TRANQUIL MOON — lemon and white	FRANCES KENT — cream and pink	HELEN COLLINGWOOD — light and dark blue	CHAR-MAIZE — beige yellow	SABLE — black violet	GREAT LAKES — medium blue	PARTY DRESS — deep coral pink	DESERT SONG — cream	CAHOKIA — pale blue

Provision has been made for 50 inexpensive varieties, covering the whole range of iris colors. Allowing 2 x 1½ feet for clumps of 3 of each variety, this would take a space 20 x 7½ feet. If desired, substitution may be made from Appendix I of more recent and therefore more costly varieties, some of them new in color.

THE IRIS BORDER

There is much to be said for giving up some place in the garden exclusively to tall bearded varieties and planning an all iris border. This may be only along one side of a path, with an appropriate background of wall or shrubbery. Such positions in small or large gardens are excellent for the display of a collection of irises, whose value in the garden is enhanced by seeing them close by and also stretched over some distance rather than densely massed.

There are likewise advantages in a double border with the appeal which balanced plantings will always have for many gardeners. In a long narrow city lot this might be along both sides of a main path leading from the house to an open lawn; even better, because irises will be in bloom for a relatively short time in the summer, it might be towards the rear of the lot, where it would be less conspicuous after blooming season. In larger places such double-bordered paths can often be planned on secondary axes or on a path leading from one part of the place devoted to a particular purpose or garden to another, for instance, from a tennis court to a rose garden.

BACKGROUNDS AND PATHS

In either case there is the consideration of backgrounds which will not detract from the beauty of the planting but enhance it and make of it a composition or picture. Most of us have to take what we find in the way of walls for background; obviously those of red brick are a problem which only time or a warm white paint can solve. In American gardens walls of stone are rare. More likely we are faced with the problem of planting in front of a stucco or tight-board fence. If the former is finished a pleasant cream and the latter a light gray, this is about as good as we can do. It will be desirable to break up the large uniform surfaces with a few shrubs or climbers.

Where no walls exist, hedges or preferably backgrounds of shrubs and small trees planted well back of the areas to be devoted to irises provide interesting texture and color in front of which irises will show to better advantage than in the open. Because the shrubs and trees for such a planting will naturally be quite different in the varying climates of the continent, it seems wise to make only general recommendations. This matter of live backgrounds is one of the most controversial subjects I have met in iris literature. It is my persuasion that as a considerable proportion of the shrubs and trees are flower-bearing it is best that the planting be made up either of those which flower before the iris season or after it. By this arrangement there is no competition for attention between the irises and the flowers of the background. Just imagine a planting of spiraeas, snowballs, weigelias, and lilacs back of an iris planting, all in flower at the same time, and my point will be recognized! Some gardeners strongly favor hedges of lilacs for planting behind irises on the theory that as the lilacs carry many of the iris colors to a higher level they enhance the beauty of the plan. English growers particularly dislike this combination and draw attention to the unsuitability of harsh green lilac foliage as a background for irises. There seems to be general agreement that a good proportion of gray foliage, evergreen or deciduous, is desirable as it picks up the glaucous quality of the iris leaves. It is also well to include some of the red and bronze foliage obtainable from Japanese maples, purple forms of barberries, and small trees of the flowering plums, Prunus Pissardii and P. Blireana, and such crab apples as Pyrus aldenhamensis and P. Eleyi. In a double iris border I once had in California—now planted to daffodils—I used in the back planting the tall Cistus ladaniferus, the medium Cistus purpureus, and the comparatively low white-flowered Cistus corbariensis—three rock-roses from the South of France with gray-green foliage of various textures. There were also many hybrid blooms of thin foliage of a grayish green, several species of the California native ceanothus, some of the green and more of the reddish-leaved forms of Leptospermum scoparium, and a number of the red or bronze-leaved crab apples. These plantings, flowering almost entirely before the irises were really well in bloom, extended backward the period of interest of the border.

There are doubtless still gardens where the labor cost of maintaining broad grass paths has not deterred the owners from keeping that most attractive of all approaches to a flower border. However, with gardeners everywhere facing the expense of maintenance, the gravel or the flag path of low upkeep is supplanting grass even where grass is easy to grow. Some paths are particularly suited to having margins of low-growing perennials which are also appropriate to the edges of an iris border as they provide the broken irregular lines which are a foil to the rigid uprightness of iris foliage. Besides, these colorful edges add interest to the border, often flowering before irises and extending beyond their season, picking up the colors of the showier flowers on a lower level and a smaller scale. Edging plants should all be easy doers. There are many to select—the varied strains of Dianthus plumarius in pinks, whites, and reds; Alyssum saxatile in a deep yellow, and particularly its paler form, Alyssum saxatile citrinum; Arabis albida; the gray-leaved lavender-flowered Nepeta Mussinii; thymes in various shades and with interesting foliage; aubrietias in wide range of iris colors, mainly lavenders, pinks, and purples; the evergreen little sunroses or helianthemums, in reds, yellows, pinks, and white; Phlox subulata in a variety of colors including a lovely grayish blue; the pink Phlox camlaensis, happiest of all dwarf phloxes in California; and violas in their wide variety of color.

AN ORIENTAL-RUG COMPOSITION

Within the borders the irises themselves should be arranged in beautiful groups which enhance each other's beauty and keep apart those obviously incompatible in color. (This special problem will be considered later in this chapter.) Here I merely suggest that excellent general effects can be achieved on what might be called an oriental-rug pattern. This can be done by setting throughout the border plants of one color as motif or binder—cream or pale yellow in one case, light blue in another, possibly pink since there are now many inexpensive varieties of that color—filling in with whatever varieties the gardener possesses, so long as studied arrangements and unpleasant clashes are avoided. In any case the taller varieties must usually be placed toward the rear, the shorter ones nearest the paths, and those of medium height in the middle rank. To obtain variety and get away from the feeling of a floral grandstand a few exceptions should be made, an occasional taller variety advanced and a group of shorter ones allowed to get into the middle area.

Gardeners with large collections of irises are sometimes worried by the spotty look at the beginning of the season, and even more by the scattered clumps of late varieties coming into bloom amid the fading flowers of earlier ones. If as far as their stature permits the late-flowering varieties are concentrated towards the front of the border so that they will screen the faded flower stems of earlier varieties at the rear, the garden effect will certainly last longer and the owner will have the pleasure of having something to show the visitor at the end of the season.

As some spaces should be left, not only between the rhizomes in a clump but particularly between groups of different varieties, a few suggestions are made for filling in temporarily until the growing irises cover the whole area. Of spring-flowering bulbs, the tall tulips are best adapted to this use; of the summer-flowering bulbs, gladiolus are fine because they do not shade the ground. Among annuals, which may be sown in fall in some parts of the country, a good strain of linaria scattered around will give a dainty lacy effect. The California poppy, in colors other than the wild orange form, will also fill in nicely; there are pleasant warm creamy whites, pinks, and rose colors which have not the arrogance in the garden of the native sons.

For summer bloom, again because they have sparse lower growth and therefore will not shade the rhizomes, the tall annual larkspurs, in white, pink, rose, blue, and purple, or the tall snapdragons in their great variety of colors will be excellent fillers. Among perennials for this temporary use it is desirable to interplant only with those which are happiest when they are started each year from offsets from old clumps; Michaelmas daisies and the fall chrysanthemums are good, and between them could very well fill up the border in its leaner years.

FOR BEARDED IRISES ONLY

A nearly all-year iris garden may well be in the main stream of the garden with the tall bearded irises followed by others which carry interest well into midsummer. But where gardens are wholly composed of the tall beardeds there is much to be said for placement off the principal line of traffic. In a narrow city lot this will be obviously at the extreme rear, as that is the only area which can be overlooked when the iris season is past.

In a larger garden the place set apart for the bearded irises may vary greatly. If the space selected is level, some formal arrangement is indicated: an open central area with beds about five feet wide and preferably of considerable length, arranged symmetrically to occupy the space, which could be screened by shrubs and trees, if not already set apart from the more open sections. I have in mind a garden in Victoria, British Columbia, which now occupies the space to the rear and somewhat above the house, where there was a tennis court when the children were young. Now sheltered and somewhat isolated, it has been developed into a garden exclusively for tall bearded irises, to be visited in its season or easily by-passed when out of flower. Where irregularities of ground present the gardener with a bowl or amphitheater or swale he is very fortunate.

This natural lay of the ground, with its excellent drainage, is not only highly acceptable to irises as a place to grow, but the contours provide perfect facilities for the display of the flowers, making backgrounds unnecessary. I still remember, though it was about thirty-five years ago that I visited it, the iris bowl in the garden of Mrs. Horatio Gates Lloyd near Philadelphia as the most effective I had ever seen for the display of a large collection of bearded irises.

These are not happy in certain situations: they do not endure shade and still flower; they are not adapted to wild gardening, for they will not stand neglect or weeds and grass growing over the rhizomes; and as they are flowers of the hillsides and mountains and dry places rather than of marshes, they should not be planted on the margins of pools or streams which are appropriate situations for the moisture-loving beardless species.

CONSIDER THE COLOR RANGE

As the value of the modern tall bearded irises is due to their extraordinary color range, consideration of the most pleasing effects from various combinations of color is desirable. In the location of plantings the lay of the land and other factors affecting the light on the flower should be studied. An open iris garden is hardly at its best in the middle of bright clear sunny days when the light is hard and clear, but in early morning, late afternoon, or in overcast weather the flowers are lovely. Under brilliant sunshine nearly all blends of pink and yellow, orange and brown, many of the reds, and even some yellows fade or burn quite badly. Some shade is valuable since it intensifies the colors of the blues, while the sunshine of late afternoon shining through makes pink irises pinker and illuminates the reds in a way to transform them. It is not always possible to select it, but in many places an eastern slope has advantages where color is concerned.

Much has been written on the subject of color by artists and gardeners, even by iris specialists. Various approaches have been made by specialists, the commonest being to start with the primary colors, red, yellow, and blue, and to derive from their combinations rules for the association in harmonies or in contrasts of the infinitely varied secondary and tertiary colors. To the mere gardener like myself, the most intelligible of these writings is the paper by Dr. Franklin Cook called "The Iris Rainbow," in *The Iris, an Ideal Hardy Perennial*, written and published by members of the American Iris Society, 1947. To this I unblushingly acknowledge my debt.

In the bearded irises we still lack a primary blue, though we are getting nearer to it. In the so-called reds we are still far from the primary color, but in the yellows we are getting close to it in such varieties as Golden Sunshine. Our iris gardens, however, are made up mainly of secondary colors, enough of them being of pure tones to be easy to handle and satisfying to the eye. Muddy blends, clouded and over-patterned plicatas, and the violent contrasts of the variegatas present problems which suggest they be a small part of any iris composition, perhaps best planted somewhere by themselves for whatever satisfaction closer examination may give.

It is the wide range of blues which makes an iris garden so attractive and blues combine best with whites, creams, pinks, and light yellows. A light blue such as Great Lakes, for example, looks well with one of the warmer whites and one of the lemon yellows, while a deeper blue, such as Chivalry, is happily associated with Bryce Canyon, a henna-colored iris. With still darker blues, brighter yellows may be combined, and with deep purples such as Master Charles a dark yellow like Ola Kala is excellent. Such light red-purples as Elmohr need medium yellows, while the cool-hued Orchid Ruffles looks best with a lemon-yellow. With the blue selfs we may use blue bicolors like Amigo and taller varieties of either the paler blue of its standards or the deeper blue of its falls. Clear white-ground plicatas with blue edges go well with self blues of the shade of the stitching in the plicata.

The pinks of roses and peonies are near in tall bearded irises. Mary Randall is a bengal rose, June Meredith a pure deep coral pink, and there are other pleasant approaches to pink. There are three, in fact: some are cool pinks, that is they have considerable residual blue; others are warm because they are blended with yellow; the pinks with tangerine beards come closer to a true pale pink, though some such as Mary Ella and Apricot Glory have apricot tints. The cold pinks—Dreamcastle is an example—are better with light yellow and with creams; the warm pinks are good with light yellows as well as with clear blues; the pink of the tangerine-bearded group is strengthened if taller whites and as clear pure blues as we have are behind it.

Only those who gardened with irises a quarter of a century ago and had to look round for early day lilies and other yellow flowers to brighten up the planting can appreciate the tremendous value of the yellows now procurable from such creams as Bellerive and Amandine, through cool lemon-yellows like Limelight, two-toned yellows like Fair Elaine and Pinnacle, to the many deeper, richer shades culminating in Berkeley Gold and Full Reward. The paler shades are useful everywhere, much better peacemakers, as I have mentioned already, than the more insistent whites. The dark ones are fine with dark purples, Black Hills or Indiana Night, for example. Though many will differ with me, I repeat here that whites should be used with restraint, preferably with pure blues and pinks. They can of course be planted near white-ground plicatas or with white-topped amoenas, both of which pick up the white in reduced amount. The so-called reds go well with pure yellows and those, like the old but still distinct French variety Professeur Mitchell, have their wine-red brought out better by being planted with violet-blues and light yellow.

A PLACE FOR PROBLEM COLORS

Dr. Cook acknowledged his difficulty in finding appropriate places for the coppery reds, for the pastel blends, the art shades, the gray-blues and tans, for variegatas and variegata blends, and for plicatas of clouded ground and dull markings. For all of these he had little use; he would, in fact, cast them out of his garden and retain only clear distinct colors. This was altogether appropriate to his small garden where perfection was achieved in a series of pictures. He did what he wanted to and did it to perfection. But what of the iris grower who has a larger place and a more catholic taste, who likes the new iris colors and has an interest in the relatively unpopular plicata or variegata patterns?

It so happens that I grow too many irises to give their grouping the consideration it should have for perfect pictures. In my recent years of breeding I have suffered from what some would consider an aberration of interest in raising plicatas of new color patterns, in breeding blends which do not fit into color schemes, and in trying to improve variegatas, which are admittedly so dominating that they are better in segregation. One fall, using exclusively selections from my own seedlings, of which I had large enough stocks to make groups, I planted a bed some fifty feet long and twelve deep. Starting at one end with the difficult variegatas—many of them blends—I offset them with a few pale yellows and yellow-ground plicatas with red or brown markings. Following these come a lot of blends shading from browns to pinks, interplanted with cream-ground pink-edged plicatas. Fortunately I had some nice blues and whites from my latest crosses, some children of Snow Flurry and Chivalry. These I placed at the end, including in the group several plants of a white-ground blue-edged plicata of my own. In the low center, offset slightly by some small whites, I planted my selections of tangerine-bearded pinks, including two seedlings as deep in color as Fantasy. These seedlings I wanted to keep and I have arranged them in a pattern tied together by the plicatas; whether when they flower they will suggest peaceful, well-behaved children at Sunday school or a bunch of dead-end kids in action, only time will tell.

Years ago I wandered into the living room of a young art professor, one of my best friends. I seemed to recognize some of the furniture, but since my previous visit the old familiar arrangement was gone. My friend looked at me, grinned, and remarked, "Molly's been improving again." Many women find in home decoration an outlet for creative imagination denied the professional and business man whose office usually remains purely utilitarian. In the iris garden, men as well as women may share the adventure of planned planting and of experiment with color, changing the arrangement whenever the spirit moves them and incidentally sloughing off the frustrations of necessarily routine lives. To do this effectively they will have to engage in the pleasurable study of the characteristics of each new iris they add—its season of bloom, its color, its height, its most desirable associates. There is much to be said for trying out all novelties in a separate place for a couple of years. During this trial period their qualities will be learned and enough plants of each developed by increase to provide for the inclusion in the iris garden of small clumps of those varieties that seem to justify this promotion.

CHAPTER ELEVEN

What Makes a Choice Variety

Whatever the basis of selection, for fancier or the general gardener, it is essential that the varieties planted should grow well and flower freely, characteristics generally found together. No one wants irises like the once distinctive but now rarely seen Isoline, which seldom flowered in successive years, as the alternate ones were given to producing a lot of non-blooming side shoots. Nor do I care any longer to grow Shah Jehan, which took three years after I planted it to flower; it was just too poor a grower here to bother with. Both Dominion and W. R. Dykes, though as parents they produced remarkable children of satisfactory vigor, were poor growers and bloomers themselves. The susceptibility of the plant to disease or disfigurements of the foliage is another thing to be taken into consideration. Santa Fe, a beautiful bluish white, was so susceptible to leaf spot that it has disappeared from my garden, and when California Peach made a disreputable-looking patch because of some trouble with its foliage even before bloom, I decided that much as I loved its color I must get along without it.

THE FANCIER'S IRIS

The flower stem should be strong enough to stand without staking. It should be branched, not so low that the lower flowers will be hidden by foliage but at least beginning half-way up the stem, with the branches held away from it and so placed that the effect is that of a candelabrum. Otherwise the flowers are apt to crowd each other, and though the mass color effect at a distance may be satisfactory the close-up view will not be pleasant. The habit of buds to turn toward the stem rather than away from it, fortunately not common, is particularly ungraceful.

The stem should be in proper proportion to the flowers, slender and not too tall if flowers are of medium size, thicker, more widely branched and taller where flowers are large. The handsome blend, Sultan's Robe, has a stem which is much too short and crowded for the proper display of its large and beautifully shaped flowers, and even Patrician does not lift its large flowers high enough into the air. Even when such irises lack height, breeders grow them for their value as parents when combined with taller, rangier irises, and gardeners, intrigued by their shapeliness and color, plant them at the front of the border to display their individual flowers. On the other hand, the stems of some irises are disproportionately tall for the size of the flowers: Three Cheers is one example, the tangerine-bearded pink Flora Zenor another, though in a mass planting this disproportion is not evident.

For a variety to have a reasonably long blooming each head should contain two or preferably three buds to open in succession. Many varieties with less than nine buds are still grown for certain qualities, but a satisfactory iris should have at least nine buds. A number of tall, widely branched varieties have considerably more.

These qualities of stem and bud are accepted everywhere, but when it comes to the flower the iris expert has set up a series of standards which in the main have merit. They are certainly important when the iris is a show flower, though they are cheerfully disregarded by the gardener who grows only a few irises chiefly for color. The flower should be of good form and pleasing proportions.

If upper petals or standards are depressed and falls overlong and drooping the disproportion is evident, just as it is if standards are large and rounded and falls short and tucked back towards the stem. Standards should be broad and touching at the tips to suggest a dome; floppy standards are anathema, and experts generally dislike shorter upright standards which leave the center of the flower exposed, although when the marking or color of the style arms is particularly attractive this fault may be rather an advantage.

Falls should be broad like the standards; at one time there were many who liked them practically horizontal, as in Santa Barbara, but the feeling that this shortened the flower has turned the taste to falls which drop and then flare into a pleasing silhouette. One of the older varieties which first showed this form was Frieda Mohr; now it is general and found in such highly rated novelties as Helen McGregor. Falls should never be narrow or straplike, never be pinched at the base; in fact the broad haft is becoming so characteristic of modern show flowers that there is danger flowers will develop too great formality or stolidity. Some of the charm of the iris will be lost if its airiness disappears.

There are other qualities in the modern iris which are always emphasized by fanciers, substance and texture. Substance, the same as "body" in cloth refers to the thickness of the petals. However beautiful in other ways, if a flower lacks substance its beauty will be fleeting, and though occasional varieties lacking substance gain popularity because of color or other qualities (China Maid is an example) substance is continually sought by breeders. The popularity of Purissima's hardier descendants Snow Flurry, Helen McGregor, New Snow, Cliffs of Dover and Swan Ballet, to mention only a few, is evidence of the importance of substance in producing a flower of beautiful form and lasting quality.

Texture applies rather to the surface of the petals, particularly the falls, where through the introduction of Dominion blood rich velvety surfaces have appeared, or in the case of the paler flowers a silvery sheen has been developed which adds considerable charm. The well-tailored flower of fine finish and smoothness, has existed for some time and continues to be popular with many iris lovers. Others are more attracted by the recent tendency of petals to contain so much material that the edges are ruffled instead of plain. Ruffling undoubtedly adds lightness and charm, but it is a question whether crimped or laciniated edges will have more than ephemeral popularity.

In the processes of scoring and registering new irises provision is always made for fragrance. This is an elusive quality and its intensity certainly varies with the nose of the judge. Irises derived from pallidas and Asia Minor species often have an aroma of orange blossoms, rich and very pleasant; others suggest the fragrance of grapes or other fruits. Fragrance is an asset, but I doubt if many place emphasis on it in selecting varieties.

Color is also in the eye of the beholder. It is probably a physical matter which colors can be most enjoyed; certainly people differ widely in the pleasure derived from particular colors. Fashion also affects popularity; at present there is strong preference for pure whites and as pure blues as can be obtained; a few years ago it was for colorful combinations of red and yellow, yellow and pink, and other blends; still earlier, it was for clear yellows.

Whatever the color, the connoisseur likes to have it clear and clean in the case of selfs, of definite harmonies or contrast in bicolors, clear markings in plicatas, and absence of cloudiness in blends. There is now definite dislike of heavy markings on the haft of the falls; this is considered to coarsen the flower, while a smooth unmarked haft refines it. There is perhaps some danger of overrefinements. One year I flowered in my garden a seedling sent me by a friend for trial. It was a tangerine-bearded pink and the base of the falls was strongly marked with bright magenta. Maybe it was just my Celtic love of color which made it so exciting to me, but as visitors came to the garden and warmed up to its barbaric color pattern I said to myself, "Here is a flower the judges will throw into outer darkness while thousands of the unelect greet it with joy."

WHAT THE AMATEUR LIKES

The canons of selection given above are those of the connoisseur and are for the collector's garden or for exhibition. The general gardener or the beginner in irises gives little thought to these matters, and quite rightly from his standpoint selects his few irises mainly for color. He wants lots of flowers and big ones, from easily grown plants. Perhaps I can best illustrate by a personal experience.

About twenty-five years ago I raised a large vigorous and floriferous yellow named Happy Days. It undoubtedly lacked refinement but its voluptuous quality, its generosity, and good nature quickly endeared it to the average visitor to iris nurseries, and its rapid increase soon permitted sale at a popular price. Today it is never found in recommended lists and has even been adversely criticized by all the experts. Yet my neighbor Carl Salbach, a large commercial iris grower, told me he had sold more Happy Days than any other variety. In the hands of breeders everywhere it has contributed to better yellows, and from it I myself raised Fair Elaine, a flower of refinement which long made the recommended lists. Personally I greatly preferred Fair Elaine to Happy Days, but I question whether it ever had the mass appeal of its parent.

For garden decoration it is unnecessary to plant expensive novelties. There is generally an older and therefore less expensive variety which will give approximately the same color effect. This is true even of the modern tangerine-bearded pinks, where for color alone a good clump of Pink Cameo or Pink Formal, not fine flowers in themselves, will look as pink at some distance as the latest pink introduction.

What is important is that varieties bear some proportion to the area in which they are to be used. A little garden or a narrow border should not be filled with great tall irises, but these should be employed where the scale is large enough to make them appropriate.

CONSIDER THE CLIMATE

Consideration of climate will probably always be necessary in selecting the tall beardeds. Each breeder instinctively saves, propagates, and introduces those seedlings which have proved best under his particular conditions. When these are distributed as named varieties and grown in wholly different

climates they may not prove as satisfactory as in their origi-
nator's garden or under conditions very similar.

Thirty-five years ago regional differences in breeding were
far more marked than today. Often bitter criticisms arose in
colder climates or those of late freezes over the behavior of
the startling new introductions from California, bred largely
from Iris mesopotamica, a species which grew like a weed
there but could never be flowered anywhere else in America.
At this same time, when the Sass brothers in Nebraska were
doing remarkable breeding of irises for cold climates and
were naturally using Iris variegata a great deal, Californians
were critical of the Sass introductions because these resented
lack of winter cold, which interfered with their winter rest,
and the absence of the summer rain essential to derivatives of
this central European species.

In recent years the wide use by breeders all over the continent of irises developed in California, Oregon, Nebraska,
Illinois, Tennessee, and New England has so intermingled
the characteristics of the species from which the tall beardeds
are derived that many fine introductions have an adaptability
nonexistent in earlier varieties. Irises like Great Lakes,
which has Conquistador ancestry from California, Dominion
ancestry from England, and other heredity from its two unknown grandparents, get along practically everywhere.

It is still true, however, that for perfect adaptability
regional breeding is necessary. In places where Dr. Kleinsorge's beautiful blends are less happy than at home in Oregon, or where David Hall's tangerine-bearded pinks lose
something of the wonderful effect they give in his Illinois
garden, breeders use these with their own strains to produce
somewhat similar varieties better suited to local conditions.

This regional breeding is possibly the only way to get tall bearded irises which will thrive under the marginal conditions of certain parts of the southern states. Certainly it offers the best chance of developing irises that will stand the rigors of the Canadian Prairie Provinces.

SELECTION FOR HOUSE DECORATION

Then there is the problem of selecting varieties to cut for indoor decoration. Many large hybrids have such tall, heavy, widely branched stems that they can only be held upright in umbrella stands or comparable containers, and while well adapted to a church wedding, they are much too large for the average room. Selection for cutting should therefore be made from the smaller, more graceful varieties, and for dinner decoration it is desirable to grow a few of the "Table Irises," really miniatures of larger forms. (It should be remembered that blues lose color under artificial light and that cool pinks are improved by it.) Also desirable for cutting are the beautiful color-patterned plicatas, which are much better when seen close up than at a distance. It follows from all this that many of the older irises and the new lilliputs, which are smaller, less branched, but highly floriferous, are still useful as cut flowers.

It is a common complaint that the blooming time of the tall beardeds is too short. Over the United States and Canada it probably averages about a month or even less in colder parts of the continent where late springs telescope the season and give an unbelievable mass of bloom over a considerably shorter time. This is true in New England. In California the blooming period of all flowers is lengthened by the slow progress of the seasons and the cool weather which prevails along the coast in April and May.

To the general gardener the short iris season compares unfavorably with that of annuals, but for the specialists, the American Iris Society judges, and the amateur breeders it is long enough; most of them would end up in sanitariums if the strain lasted much longer. In any case, if gardeners are willing to include the minor types of bearded irises in their gardens, they can lengthen the season from the end of the daffodils to the beginning of the peonies and even arrange for a short return engagement in the autumn.

THE SMALLER BEARDED IRISES

Although dwarf bearded irises have fallen into some neglect of late (possibly because until recently American breeders have not been trying to improve them), they constitute an important group of garden plants which will start the bearded iris season at least a month earlier in most areas than their big brothers of the tall bearded section. I venture to prophesy a revival of interest in them. The founder and head of the Dwarf Iris Society, Walter Welch of Middlebury, Indiana, has just sent me a list of the 1959 DIS awards. My favorite Blue Frost got the DIS medal, and awards of special merit went to the following varieties: Angel Eyes (Jones), White Mite (Welch), Wee Blue (Welch), Tear Drops (Beattie), Burgundy Velvet (Simonson), Claire (Brown) and Flashlight (Welch). Popular among the less expensive miniature dwarf varieties are Black Baby, Blazon, Blue Band, Buster Brown, Cherry Spot, Lavender Dawn, Path of Gold, Red Gem, Promise, Verigay and Violet Gem, as well as those two century-old favorites Atroviolacea and Azurea.

Descriptions of all these will be found in the catalogues of those dealers who specialize in dwarfs. Some of these dealers are mentioned in the Appendix listing sources of supply.

Earl Roberts of Indianapolis, Indiana, president of the Median Iris Society, reports: "When the MIS was organized, we estimated it would take five years to get them (median irises) into production in any quantity, and we guessed just about right." That this production is exceptional in quality seems beyond dispute, for in 1959 in newly created categories the following recently introduced varieties received an Honorable Mention award from the American Iris Society: The standard dwarfs Blue Denim (Warburton), Dancing Bee (Roberts), Lemon Flame (Muhlstein), Lilli-Green (Welch), Lilli-Yellow (Welch), Little Cottage (Muhlstein) and Little Dogie (Roberts); and the border irises Chocoleto (Deru), Frenchi (Jones), Moontalk (Crosby), Pinata (Kleinsorge) and Two Bits (Albright). In the standard dwarf class, which seems destined to become widely popular, other highly rated varieties are already inexpensive: there are the white Brite and Lilli-White; yellow Baria, Brassie and Yellow Bantam, Pigmy Gold and Smoothy; blue Fairy Flax, Small Wonder and Tinkerbell; and purple Dark Star, Pagan Midget and Little Shadow. November and Tan Fantasy are brown bitones. Greenspot, white with a green spot, was, in 1959, the first to receive the new Cook-Douglas award. And Geddes Douglas has a pink lilliput, not yet introduced. Soon all the colors available in the tall bearded will be found in this class.

The term "intermediate" is, I believe, properly applied to a hybrid race derived from crossing the dwarf and the tall bearded irises. An English amateur, W. J. Caparne, raised a great many of these about the beginning of the century and for a time they had considerable popularity because they filled in the gap between the flowering of their parents.

The original intermediates introduced by Caparne and by Goos & Koenemann are now hard to find in catalogues. They have been largely replaced by intermediates of later American breeding. A collection of these might include Autumn Queen, white, Blue Asterisk, pale blue, blue spot, Cloud Fluff, white, Chrysoro, deep yellow, Florinda, violet, Marine Wave, navy blue and Ruby Glow, red. Cook's Kiss-Me-Kate, a cream, bordered blue, Craig's amethyst-gray Moonchild, and Jonas' two flamingo pinks, Pink Debut and Pink Elf, are still expensive novelties. I myself now grow only the very distinct and rather dwarf intermediate white, Snow Maiden, which for groups or drifts has in my opinion no competitor in its season. Like most California gardeners I have lost interest in the intermediates because we here have certain tall bearded irises which overlap with the intermediates in season and surpass them in beauty and individuality. In nearly all other parts of the continent the intermediates really do bridge a gap, and justify their inclusion in a good-sized garden.

SELECTING TALL BEARDED IRISES

As there are now literally hundreds of tall bearded irises offered in American catalogues, not to mention the English and French varieties, it is a rash individual who would put into a book as the "best" a small selection of these. It could in any case be only a personal choice. Many years ago in an article I wrote for *Bailey's Cyclopedia of American Horticulture* I attempted such a list from the then relatively few good varieties. Last year a facetious friend sent me a copy of this old list, which does not contain a single variety offered by American growers today. Progress in breeding is now so rapid that varieties are quickly superseded by better ones of the same color. The wise beginner will make his initial choice by looking through several catalogues or, preferably, by visiting iris nurseries and private collections where he can learn which are the early, mid-season, and late varieties so as to extend his season; which are short or tall, and which are best in the particular colors that appeal to him.

For the collector, however, I have reproduced as an Appendix the American Iris Society's Symposium of 1959, a list of the hundred most highly rated varieties arranged first according to their rank and then separately by color. These are, of course, mainly very recent introductions. Many are still highly priced because demand is still greater than supply. I am therefore giving below a much shorter list. The following seventeen varieties are widely grown; most have received Awards of Merit from the American Iris Society.

I give merely the names, breeders, and dates of introduction, with brief color notes:

WHITE: New Snow (Fay, '46), White Sprite (Cassebeer, '51)
CREAM: Amandine (Douglas, '46), Desert Song (Fay, '46)
YELLOW: Cloth of Gold (Whiting, '45), Leading Lady (Lyell, '50)
PINK: Happy Birthday (D. Hall, '52), Helen Louise (Lapham, '52)
RED: Cordovan (Keinsorge, '46)
BROWN: Argus Pheasant (DeForest, '48)
TAN BLEND: Cascade Splendor (Kleinsorge, '43)
ORCHID: Pink Plume (Schreiner, '51)
LIGHT BLUE: Distance (Cook, '46), Helen McGregor (Graves, '46)
MEDIUM BLUE: Chivalry (Wills, '44), Pierre Menard (Faught, '48)
BLUE BLACK: Black Hills (Fay, '51)

Mention should be made here of the annual award of the Dykes Memorial Medal, one each for American, British, and French introductions. Of recent years the American awards have certainly gone to irises of real distinction; but in the past, both here and abroad, there has been considerable controversy as to the wisdom of the choices made and a list of winners of this medal would not today constitute a satisfactory buying list.

FALL-BLOOMING IRISES

A few years ago an amateur iris grower in Chattanooga, Tennessee, said that he would soon be able to invite iris lovers to a great show of bloom in autumn in his garden. There had already been developed, largely by selection from irises of the Intermediate group, a number of varieties which under favorable conditions of climate and culture could be pretty well depended on to flower in September, October, and even into early November. Although there have been additions to this list since then, it must be acknowledged that advancement in the breeding of dependable fall bloomers has not been rapid, possibly because the demand for them is not constant.

Among these repeaters or re-bloomers, for they have their normal flowering season in spring, certain varieties can be recommended as fairly sure to perform, given favorable conditions: Autumn Queen, white; Autumn Elf, cream and lilac; Autumn Sunset, pink blend; Autumn Flame, red; Double Date, yellow; Eleanor Roosevelt, violet; and San Grael, yellow. These, with the exception of Autumn Flame, are relatively short-stemmed, up to about two feet. Autumn

Haze, violet, and Martie Everest, blue, are considerably taller.

Climatically the fall bloomers are not adapted to Canada or the cold northern states, where September or early October frosts would catch them in bud, but from New York to Pennsylvania, Virginia, and westward through Iowa and Kansas, where killing frosts come later, they have proved more successful and popular. The fall bloomers are naturally varieties of vigorous growth and rapid increase, which do not need a summer rest. To get the best results from them, better than average culture is required. They must be watered and fed to promote the growth of the new rhizomes from which the fall flowers are to come, and as they must be rapid propagators they need more frequent division than other varieties. This should be done immediately after spring flowering.

In California one rarely finds the varieties classed as fall bloomers. This may be due in part to the length of the spring iris season, satisfying most growers. Furthermore, if Californians want fall bloom it is possible for them to select certain tall bearded irises which under their conditions will bloom fairly regularly twice a year if they get early fall rains or irrigation. Even where no attempt whatever was made to induce fall flowering, I have observed that such varieties as California Gold, Radiant, Sultan's Robe, Lady Mohr, Narada, and others often bloom a second time in fall in Berkeley. In Los Angeles, Tom Craig, by superior culture and summer watering, seems to be able to flower many varieties, including Ball Gown, Cupid's Dart and Savage, all through autumn and early winter. To some of us fall bloomers do not seem desirable. To me the tall bearded iris is a flower of light, with its predominance of whites, light blues, and other colors which suggest spring or early summer. I do not want chrysanthemums in iris time, nor do I much care for irises in chrysanthemum time; to the latter, with their rich yellows, bronzes, and reds, belongs the autumn.

CHAPTER TWELVE

Aril Irises: Oncocyclus and Regelias

The name aril comes from the little white collar, or aril, found on the seeds of all species in this group.

Native to Asia Minor, Syria, the Caucasus, and western Persia, the oncocyclus is not a true bearded iris, but so closely related that it is now classified as a pogon. By far the greatest number of species grow in Palestine, among them the strangest, weirdest, and most beautiful of all irises. These may have been the native "lilies of the field" referred to in the Bible. If so, it was probably no exaggeration that "Solomon in all his glory was not arrayed like one of these."

The oncocyclus species are little known or grown in America, as they have proved singularly difficult under our conditions. At times, due to the turmoil in the Near East, it has been impossible for collectors to gather rhizomes where found in nature, practically the only source of supply. Up to and more easily since World War II, it has been possible to import from C. G. Van Tubergen, Haarlem, Holland. Now, from Gevin Bulb Nurseries of Israel (through their American agent Marjorie Anthes of Encinatas, Calif.), many of these irises are obtainable at such reasonable prices that, though they flowered but once or twice and then died out, enthusiasts were willing to replace them.

English gardeners, always adventurous, were the pioneers in the culture of oncocyclus and many Americans grew several species for a number of years. A very few growers, even though they lost their original importations, succeeded in making crosses between the different species, though most of these, too, eventually perished. Clarence White, of Redlands, California, for many years flowered annually beautiful seedlings of oncocyclus ancestry. Frank Reinelt, of Capitola, raised in his garden on the central California coast several hundred oncocyclus seedlings which he grew on and flowered in a friend's garden in the foothills of the Sierras, a climate which apparently approaches their natural conditions. When I saw them in the 1930s there were hundreds of clumps, each with ten or a dozen flower spikes, truly a marvelous sight. However, when these were moved back to the coast, with its damp winters and cool summers, they were all lost. In my comparable Berkeley climate I managed to flower Iris susiana, I. Gatesii, and several other species but could not keep them permanently.

THE MOURNING IRIS

The one oncocyclus which has persisted in cultivation for nearly four hundred years is Iris susiana. Originally it was assumed that this iris came from Persia, but now it is considered a form of basaltica, a species native to Palestine. Iris susiana has been successfully grown for a while at least by many American gardeners. It has even been shown in the windows of florists, where its huge, rather funereal flowers—the effect of a gray ground heavily lined and stippled with dark purple and a characteristic cushion of purple hairs replacing the linear beard of the true pogonirises—have excited tremendous interest. It is sometimes called the "mourning" iris, and some would question its true beauty, which is somewhat macabre.

In nature a number of the oncocyclus irises, including susiana, come from parts of Palestine not far from Egypt where the only rains start them into growth in winter. They flower in early spring and shortly afterwards go dormant to enjoy a thorough baking from the hot sun of the rainless summer. More of the desirable species, however, and this includes Iris Gatesii, I. Lortetii, and I. iberica, come from the mountainous regions of the Lebanon, the Caucasus, Armenia, and Kurdistan, where they are frozen and completely covered with snow all winter, make all their growth, flower in the short spring, and then go dormant to be thoroughly ripened by the summer drought. Such conditions are almost impossible for gardeners in this country to approximate. If there were enthusiasts in the high Sierras of California or the mountains in Arizona or New Mexico, it might be possible for them to duplicate such conditions, but in the lowlands where most of us have gardens, with open winters in California and wet summers in the eastern half of North America, establishing these irises seems almost impossible. Yet they are grown commercially in normally moist Holland, and iris fanciers everywhere who have fallen under the spell of their strange beauty will keep trying to grow them. An increasing interest in growing and breeding arils may be indicated by the formation of The Aril Society International in California in 1955.

When well-ripened rhizomes could be imported they often flowered the succeeding spring but showed a distressing tendency to decline thereafter. It was not simply a matter of winter cold as is sometimes assumed, for F. Cleveland Morgan reported some years ago that he had flowered Iris susiana in his garden near Montreal in the season following importation but that it refused to mature even if lifted during the summer months. This procedure of lifting the peculiar reddish-skinned, somewhat stoloniferous rhizomes in early summer and drying them off in a warm greenhouse or other sheltered sunny place has been recommended by English growers and also successfully used by Americans. One correspondent so grew Iris susiana in Iowa and reported some success in keeping this difficult plant. The practice of covering the beds with glass frames in summer to shed rain has also been tried, but without success, as what the rhizomes want is a more thorough baking and drying than this gives in most American climates. Though growing naturally in heavy clay soil, it is desirable in gardens to give these irises a rich soil with plenty of dolomitic limestone in it and preferably to make raised beds so as to insure drainage. In climates of hot arid summers no lifting is necessary.

ONCOCYCLUS TRAITS

It would be futile to devote much space to descriptions of these beautiful, difficult, and largely unprocurable irises. I shall only describe them briefly and mention two or three which have importance because they have been used in the breeding of comparatively easy garden plants. The foliage of the oncocyclus irises is characteristically short and sickle-shaped rather than upright. There are many flower stems to a clump, varying in height from a few inches up to nearly two feet. Flowers in the different species also vary in size.

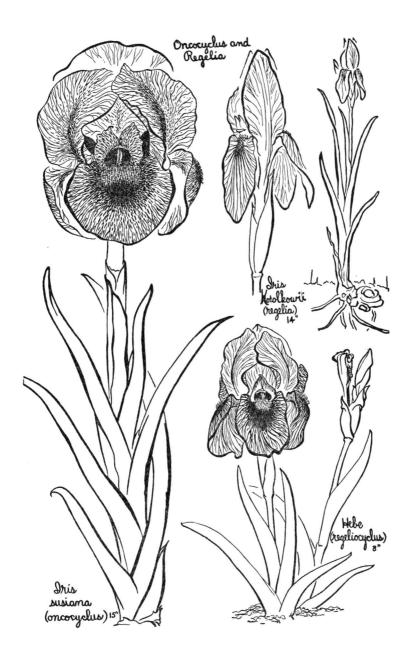

Oncocyclus and
Regelia

Iris
Kotolkowii
(regelia)
14"

Iris
susiana
(oncocyclus) 15"

Hebe
(regeliocyclus)
8"

Each stem carries but a single bloom of rounded form and often of relatively large size for its leafage and stature.

Iris iberica, from the Caucasus, generally has flowers with white standards and falls covered with brown-purple veins, on stems only about six inches in height. Iris Lortetii, from the southern slopes of Lebanon, has been claimed to be the most beautiful of all irises. Its single flowers are carried on stems about a foot high; they have large white-veined violet standards, and rounded falls finely dotted with crimson on a creamy ground with a beautiful blotch of crimson at the base of each. Iris Samariae, from Palestine, is much like Lortetii, but when grown in California, Samariae was larger and more vigorous. Iris Gatesii was once supposed to have the largest flowers of any iris—this was before the production of the huge hybrids of today. As I saw it in England and grew it in my own garden years ago, it was a great rounded flower of pale gray-white with fine purplish venation and stippling, the markings so toned down that the effect was beautiful, almost ghostly. Of these three, iberica is important as being the seed-parent of the easily grown hybrid Ibmacrantha, and Gatesii because from it was raised the hybrid William Mohr, the progenitor of a new race of easy culture.

There are many more oncocyclus iris species, solid dark purples like I. atropurpurea, flowers with yellow ground like I. auranitica, both Palestinian species which are now available from Lloyd Austin, Placerville, California.

THE REGELIAS

In Russian Turkestan occur a few closely related iris species of easier culture. These have been grouped as the regelia section. The three species which I have grown and with which many gardeners have had success from the colder climates of the Atlantic Coast to California, where they are reasonably permanent, are Korolkowii, stolonifera, and Hoogiana. They are available by import and may be found in the catalogues of a few commercial iris growers in the United States and Canada. Under conditions of good well-drained soil on the alkaline side and a thorough summer rest such as they get in semiarid climates (or can be given by protection or lifting), regelias not only thrive but increase, though occasional losses occur. Their reddish rhizomes are less compact than those of the oncocyclus and they spread fairly rapidly by stolons, so that occasional replanting is advisable. Doubtless the fact that they remain dormant through the autumn is a reason for their easy culture in cold climates.

Iris Korolkowii, with a more compact rhizome than the other two, has stems of fifteen to eighteen inches with a head of two or more flowers, varying in color from a creamy white with heavy purple lines to a reddish purple ground with less conspicuous veining. They are relatively long narrow flowers, with pointed segments. Iris stolonifera is usually some shade of brown lighted up by blue in the center of the petals, the edges frilled, and the general effect so crisp that the flowers seem made of metal as they stand about eighteen inches high and above the slender foliage. W. R. Dykes raised a hybrid between Korolkowii and stolonifera which he called Turkoman and which I commend for its uniform ruby-red and beautifully contrasting blue beard; this is apparently the variety now listed by Van Tubergen as Lucia.

Utterly different is Hoogiana, the most perfectly finished, beautifully tailored flower in the whole iris family. Larger than either of the others, it bears lovely clear blue flowers on stems two feet or more in height. There are also larger forms than the type, some with a purplish tone, but with less perfection, as I grew them, than the type. This is the easiest of the regelias and has been successfully grown under ordinary culture by many gardeners.

REGELIOCYCLUS HYBRIDS

Though others—for example Sir Michael Foster in England and William Mohr in California—made crosses between members of the regelia and the oncocyclus groups in efforts to produce a garden race combining their characteristics but with the comparative ease of culture of the regelias, it was the Dutch firm of Van Tubergen which did most work in this field. They alone introduced the hybrids into commerce and after nearly half a century are still growing many of them. While none have the great size or rounded form of the parent oncocyclus, the flowers are much larger than the regelias and many have attractive and distinctive patterns and markings. Among named ones some are too similar, but any selection should include a variety such as Camilla, Eunice, Homerus, or Luna, with gray ground and violet veining, one of the varieties like Charon or Isolde, which have a bronzy mahogany ground with gold veining, a uniform ruby-red like Asperina, and a soft violet like Ulysses. These do not cover the whole range of colors. The flowers of all are beautiful, lifted up on stems a foot to eighteen inches high; all have two buds to the flower head, like the regelias. In California, Lloyd Austin has introduced a number of these hybrids including Persian Bronze and Persian Twotone; and Herbert Kerr's unnamed hybrid seedlings are available from Melrose Gardens, Modesto.

These regeliocyclus irises prefer a reasonably rich, well-drained soil with lime in it and fertilizer well below the rhizome. They are pretty indifferent to winter cold where protected by snow, but they like a good baking and drying out in summer. They are reported to be easily managed in a garden near Montreal if, after the foliage dies down, the rhizomes are lifted and stored in sand in flats in a greenhouse during the late summer months, and then replanted in light sandy soil towards the end of October. Near London, Ontario, there have been permanent plantings where this procedure is followed and hundreds of flowers are produced each year. While teaching at the University of Michigan years ago I saw large patches of these hybrids in bloom. Here the owner said they had been flowering, unmoved for years, probably because of extraordinarily fine drainage and summer drought, as this garden was underlaid by a terminal moraine. Where the summer is dry, no lifting is necessary. Provided the suggested cultural conditions are met, regeliocyclus irises are nearly as easy to grow as the tall beardeds.

ONCOPOGONS OR ONCOBREDS

Iris breeders, mainly enthusiastic amateurs, have long sought to combine the startling colorings of the oncocyclus irises with the ease of culture of the pogon or true-bearded irises. Such crosses are difficult to make and the seeds are hard to germinate. Iris susiana many years ago was crossed with a dwarf bearded iris and gave the early flowering Zwanenburg, a gray and yellow flower, more interesting than beautiful; and from the Sass brothers in Nebraska came Balradour and other dwarfs which were the results of comparable crosses. Sir Michael Foster raised many hybrids between various oncocyclus and Iris pallida, but these have largely disappeared from catalogues as they were all rather dark and without the distinctive beauty of the oncocyclus irises. Van Tubergen's Ibmacrantha, a cross between the oncocyclus iberica and the tall bearded macrantha or amas, is little grown excepting for breeding purposes.

The great break in this breeding occurred about thirty-five years ago when William Mohr in his garden at Mount Eden, California, succeeded in getting a single seed from a cross of Iris Gatesii by the bearded Iris Parisiana. In 1923 he flowered the pale manganese-violet, finely lined and of beautiful shape and huge size, which, after his untimely death, I named William Mohr and introduced into commerce. It proved quite hardy and in its early years flourished in climates as cold as Winnipeg or as warm as Redlands. Apparently much of the stock in later years has been affected by mosaic and lost its vigor, though Colorado growers are reputed still to have healthy plants. From William Mohr as seed-parent, breeders have raised the next generation with the pollen of tall bearded irises, though the oncocyclus characteristics are less noticeable in such derivatives as Ormohr, Elmohr, Mohr Courageous and Mohr Majesty.

These characteristics are returning in the latest of the hybrids, where the pollen parent, Capitola, raised by Frank Reinelt from crossing William Mohr with Ibmacrantha, is used on tall bearded seed-parents. Lloyd Austen's outstanding Real Gold comes from Capitola, and Jack Linse has used this same parent with remarkable success. The vigorous Lady Mohr, (raised by Carl Salbach), with oyster-white standards, chartreuse falls, and some crimson markings in the throat, is after sixteen years still distinctive among the newer hybrids. The recently introduced Trophy (Linse '58) and Mohr Haven (Reynolds '57) revive the lighter effects of the oncocyclus in distinctive blues. The end is not in sight, for breeders all over America are working on this combining of oncocyclus and tall bearded iris. Outstanding among them for many years was the late Clarence White, of Redlands, who developed his own strain of what he called "oncobreds" and produced, among many distinctive and relatively easily grown varieties, the tall and strangely colored Joppa Parrot, the beautiful little Some Love (which recalls I. Lortetii), and the alluring Present. His influence will be felt indefinitely in this breeding, for, in addition to his many oncobred introductions, he succeeded in producing from pure oncocyclus crosses, tetraploid varieties (Beisan Aga, Asoka of Nepal, etc.) which Jack Linse, Fred Crandall, Tell Muhlstein and others are using in their breeding. Tom Craig, of Escondido, has already raised from Purissima by Capitola the still lovely dark blue Peg Dabagh, the handsome medium blues Heigho and Mary Valentine, and from Snow Flurry by Capitola the huge gray-lavender Frances Craig, and has thousands of seedlings which will doubtless add to the variation in this race. I have heard very favorable reports on the recently introduced varieties Mohr Lemonade (Muhlstein, '58), which contains some regelia blood, and Witch Doctor (Plough, '55) though I have not yet seen them. The new Troy Meadows (deFussi, '59) and Wind Shadows (Conrad, '59) are, according to an enthusiastic correspondent, "sensational."

The culture of these oncopogons is quite similar to that of the tall beardeds and those derived from William Mohr, like Elmohr and Lady Mohr, are quite as vigorous, floriferous, easy of culture, and free of increase as the pure tall bearded irises.

REGELIABREDS

Much less has been done with combining the regelias and the bearded irises. From such combinations Mr. Mohr raised the attractive blue Carmelo, the mouse-colored Bellorio, and the distinctive Raspberry, all easy to grow but because of their narrow petals and shyness of bloom now rarely found. Tell Muhlstein produced from I. Hoogiana the three brilliantly blue hybrids Blue Fairy, Hoogie-Boy and Little Lake; and Fred Crandall crossed the old blue Shining Waters with the same species for the tall shingling blue Rainier Valley. From England have come two recent hybrids from I. stolonifera; Mr. Benbow's blue and lavender Saffron Charm (1954) and Mr. Fothergill's electric blue Silken Dalliance (1958). There are, however, still opportunities for breeding along theses lines. Walter Marx in Oregon has recently been combining the regelia species with the dwarf bearded irises to get a strain of early and distinctive flowers, and Stanley Street has crossed an arenaria hybrid with Andromache for Wee Scot (1959), a violet bitone with a dark signal patch.

American Iris Society's
Popularity Poll - 1959
The Twentieth Official Symposium

The Hundred Favorite Bearded Irises of the United States and Canada are in order of popularity—

1 Blue Sapphire	35 Thotmes III	68 Golden Garland
2 Violet Harmony	36 Tranquility	69 Snow Goddess
3 Mary Randall	37 Regina Maria	70 White Peacock
4 Truly Yours	38 Blue Shimmer	71 Native Dancer
5 Palomino	39 Desert Song	72 Beechleaf
6 Happy Birthday	40 Minnie Colquitt	73 Temple Bells
7 Sable Night	41 Galilee	74 Carmela
8 First Violet	42 Wabash	75 Cherie
9 June Meredith	43 Sierra Skies	76 Great Lakes
10 Limelight	44 Taholah	77 Helen Collingwood
11 Pierre Menard	45 Lady Ilse	78 Chantilly
12 Swan Ballet	46 Harbor Blue	79 Dotted Swiss
13 Black Hills	47 Char-Maize	80 Lady Rogers
14 Inca Chief	48 Eleanor's Pride	81 Gold Sovereign
15 Pinnacle	49 Whole Cloth	82 Crispette
16 Argus Pheasant	50 Zantha	83 Melodrama
17 Chivalry	51 Cahokia	84 Wedding Bouquet
18 Frost and Flame	52 Cloudcap	85 Foxfire
19 Black Taffeta	53 Dreamy	86 Lynn Hall
20 Ola Kala	54 Port Wine	87 Apricot Glory
21 Cliffs of Dover	55 Spanish Peaks	88 Ballerina
22 Elmohr	56 Jane Phillips	89 Belle Meade
23 Rehobeth	57 May Hall	90 Big Game
24 Starshine	58 Party Dress	91 Cascade Splendor
25 Frances Craig	59 Helen McGregor	92 Amethyst Flame
26 Lady Mohr	60 Caroline Jane	93 Storm Warning
27 New Snow	61 Deep Black	94 Patrician
28 Top Flight	62 Melody Lane	95 Pink Formal
29 Blue Rhythm	63 Queen's Lace	96 Fleeta
30 Cascadian	64 Majorette	97 Golden Russet
31 Techny Chimes	65 Solid Gold	98 Mystic Melody
32 Butterscotch Kiss	66 Amandine	99 Lavanesque
33 Snow Flurry	67 Sable	100 Mulberry Rose
34 Cathedral Bells		

COLOR CLASSIFICATION OF THE SAME HUNDRED
FAVORITES OF 1959

(The number following each variety gives its rank in the symposium)

White
Swan Ballet (12), Frost and Flame (18), Cliffs of Dover (21), New
Snow (27), Cascadian (30), Snow Flurry (33), Tranquility (36),
Dreamy (53), Spanish Peaks (55), Snow Goddess (69), White Peacock
(70), Wedding Bouquet (84)

Cream and Lemon
Limelight (10), Pinnacle (15), Starshine (24), Desert Song (39),
Char-Maize (47), Amandine (66), Mystic Melody (98)

Yellow and White
Truly Yours (4), Queen's Lace (63), Patrician (94)

Yellow
Techny Chimes (31), Zantha (50), Solid Gold (65), Golden Garland
(68), Gold Sovereign (81), Foxfire (85)

Yellow, Buff and Tan Blends
Butterscotch Kiss (32), Lady Mohr (26), Temple Bells (73), Car-
mela (74), Apricot Glory (87), Cascade Splendor (91), Golden Russet (97).

Brown
Argus Pheasant (16), Thotmes III (35), Beechleaf (72).

Coral, Buff and Peach Pink
Palomino (5), Happy Birthday (6), June Meredith (9), Cathedral
Bells (34), Cloudcap (52), May Hall (57), Party Dress (58), Melody
Lane (62), Native Dancer (71), Cherie (75), Lynn Hall (86), Bal-
lerina (88), Pink Formal (95), Fleeta (96).

Rose
Mary Randall (3), Mulberry Rose (100)

Light Blue and Lavender
Blue Sapphire (1), Rehobeth (23), Frances Craig (25), Galilee (41),
Sierra Skies (43), Lady Ilse (45), Harbor Blue (46), Eleanor's Pride
(48), Whole Cloth (49), Cahokia (51), Jane Phillips (56), Helen
McGregor (59), Lady Rogers (80)

Medium Blue
Pierre Menard (11), Chivalry (17), Blue Rhythm (29)
Regina Maria (37), Great Lakes (76)

Mauve, Violet and Purple
First Violet (8), Elmohr (22), Violet Harmony (2), Majorette (64), Big Game (90)

Black Violets
Sable Night (7), Black Taffeta (19), Deep Black (61), Sable (66), Storm Warning (92)

Blue Plicatas
Blue Shimmer (38), Caroline Jane (60), Dotted Swiss (79), Belle Meade (89)

Pink Plicatas
Minnie Colquitt (38), Taholah (43), Port Wine (54)

Orchid Pink and Lilac
Chantilly (78), Crispette (82), Melodrama (bitone) (82)
Amethyst Flame (92), Lavanesque (99)

Amoena and Neglecta
Wabash (42), Helen Hollingwood (77)

A Sequence of Irises

No satisfactory iris calendar for the United States and Canada can be made as the time of blooming in this great area of diverse climates varies too greatly. I have therefore appended a list of irises in the approximate order in which they usually flower. The main purpose of this is to show how by growing many species and varieties the iris season may be extended over many months—even, in favored places, through the whole year. While I have grouped the irises by seasons, here again actual blooming time will be a relative matter, depending on latitude and climatic conditions.

Winter—January to March

　　Iris alata (Outdoors in warm climates, under glass in cold ones)
　　Iris unguicularis (I. stylosa) (Outdoors in warm climates; or in cold climates protected by glass frames)
　　Iris histrioides, I. reticulata
　　Iris sindjarensis, I. bucharica, I. orchioides

Spring—April to June

　　Iris pumila
　　Iris Chamaeris and other miniature dwarf bearded varieties
　　Iris Wedgwood, followed by other "Dutch" irises
　　Iris japonica (Outdoors in warm climates, indoors in cold ones)
　　Standard dwarf bearded varieties
　　Intermediate bearded irises
　　Iris albicans, I. germanica, I. Kochii
　　Oncocyclus, Regelias, and Regeliocyclus varieties
　　Californian and Pacific Coast natives, Iris longipetala, I. Douglasiana, I. innominata, I. tenax, I. bracteata
　　"Spanish" irises (Iris xiphium and varieties)
　　Tall bearded irises, and border irises

Siberian irises
Iris fulva, I. foliosa, I. giganticærulea, Louisiana species and hybrids
Iris tectorum
Iris cristata, I. gracilipes, I. graminea, I. setosa, I. versicolor
Iris Pseudacorus
Iris chrysographes, I. Forrestii, I. Wilsonii, I. lævigata
Iris Delavayi
Spuria irises (I. ochroleuca, I. Monnieri, and hybrids)
"English irises" (Iris xiphioides)

Summer—July to September

Japanese irises (Iris Kaempferi varieties)
Iris dichotoma

Autumn—October to December

Fall blooming bearded irises, including Iris Kochii
Tall bearded irises—many varieties under California conditions
Iris unguicularis (I. stylosa) (Begins in autumn, extending into new year.)

APPENDIX III

Sources of Information

American Iris Society, 2237 Tower Grove Blvd., St. Louis 10, Mo. Annual membership $5.00. Publishes quarterly *Bulletin*. In 1959 brought out *Garden Irises,* edited by L. F. Randolph, consisting of 33 chapters (550 pages), written by specialist members for this book: price, cloth $7.95.

Joining this organization of amateur and trade growers is the best way to keep up to date with the growing iris world.

The Iris Society, the comparable English organization. Publishes *The Iris Year Book,* a fascinating and important assembly of papers international in scope. Americans may send annual membership fee, $3.00, through the American Iris Society.

The great authoritative monograph on irises is *The Genus Iris,* by W. R. Dykes, Cambridge University Press, 1913. This is an expensive work which may be found in large libraries and in the Farr Memorial Libraries of the A. I. S. *A Handbook of Garden Irises,* by W. R. Dykes, London, Hopkinson, 1924, is the best substitute for the amateur.

American garden literature has been lacking in new popular iris books in the last couple of decades. In England, *Iris Culture for Amateurs,* by R. E. Spender and L. F. Pesel, London, Country Life Ltd., 1937; *Irises, Their Culture and Selection,* by Gwendolyn Anley, London, Collingridge, 1946 and *The Iris,* by N. Leslie Cave, Chanticleer Press, Inc., 1951, meet this need.

This book is the author's attempt to provide a popular treatment for the United States and Canada.

Sources of Plants

The following list of iris growers is a purely personal one. It includes only a few general dealers who have introduced many new irises. It stresses rather those who can supply the less common species, beardless irises, and their varieties. Inclusion of all individual and trade growers is impossible and the omission of nationally known firms is no reflection on their standing.

American

Brown's Iris Garden, 14920 Hi-way 99, Lynwood, Washington. Median and miniature dwarf bearded, Siberians, Japanese, spurias, Louisiana, western species; named varieties of Dutch, English, reticulata, as well as tall bearded irises, including exclusive introductions.

Chatauqua Flowerfield, Greenhurst, N. Y. Bearded, Japanese, and named varieties of Iris xiphioides (English iris).

Combsie's Iris and Bulb Gardens. Dwarf, median and tall bearded, oncobreds, spurias, Louisianas, and the Pacific Coast native hybrid originations of Johnson and Luhrsen. Japanese, too, though not listed.

Cooley's Gardens, Silverton, Ore. Bearded irises: introducer of Kleinsorge varieties.

Tom Craig, 910 Rome Drive, Rt. 4, Box 315, Escondido, Calif. Besides bearded irises, grows many oncocyclus hybrids, beardless species, and varieties.

Easy Breeze Gardens, 1421 N. 16th Ave., Yakima, Washington. Linse introductions of oncobreds and tall bearded, plus general list.

Edenwald Gardens, Vincennes, Indiana. Features the less expensive Payne originations of Japanese irises, plus Siberian and tall bearded.

Fairmont Gardens, Lowell, Mass. Bearded irises including many exclusive introductions; Siberians, Louisiana irises, evansias.

Flowerfield Bulb Farm, Flowerfield, Long Island, N. Y. Good list of Iris Kaempferi varieties; includes Dutch, English, and a few species irises.

J. N. Giridlian, Oakhurst Gardens, Arcadia, Calif. Not exclusively an iris dealer, but offers many evansias and some other species.

Lyon Iris Gardens, Van Nuys, Calif. Bearded, Spuria, and Pacific Coast native varieties.

Walter Marx Gardens, Boring, Ore. Besides bearded irises—tall, intermediate, dwarf—and a fine list of Japanese irises, offers many unusual things, regelias and regeliocyclus, bulbous irises, and miscellaneous species including Pacific Coast natives and others difficult to find in America.

Melrose Gardens, Modesta, Calif. Bearded irises, new and antique, tall, dwarf and median; oncocyclus and oncobreds, spurias, Louisianas, laevigatas, Dutch, Spanish, reticulatas, junos. Fascinating catalogue.

Moldovan's Gardens, 4121 Russell St., Lorain, Ohio. Selected list of new bearded irises—talls, miniature dwarfs, standard dwarfs and intermediates.

W. A. Payne, R.R.3, Box 180, Terre Haute, Indiana. List of recent introductions, only, of his own originations of Japanese irises. For the collector, only.

Milliken Gardens, Arcadia, Calif. Bearded irises including Clarence White introductions and fine selection of newer spurians and Louisiana irises.

Rainbow Hybridizing Gardens, Placerville, Calif. Bearded irises, including rare oncocyclus and regelias, and Clarence White oncobreds.

Schreiner's Iris Gardens, Rte. 2, Box 297, Salem, Ore. Good descriptions and color lists of tall bearded irises including new introductions from several breeders. Interesting catalogue.

Syllmar Gardens, San Fernando, Calif. Bearded, Japanese, Siberian, Spurias, and Regeliocyclus irises.

Tell's Iris Gardens, 691 East 8th North, Provo, Utah. An indispensable catalogue: tall, median, dwarf bearded, oncobreds, including some of Clarence White's spurias, and comments.

Canadian

K. Christiansen, Saanich Road, R.M.D. 3, Victoria, B. C. No catalogue, but perhaps the best collection of beardless species in North America.

English

Barr & Sons, King St., Covent Garden, London W.C.2, England. R. W. Wallace & Co., Tunbridge Wells, England.

The above are the oldest existing English growers of bearded and species irises. The latter offers seed of some rare things.

Dutch

C. G. van Tubergen Ltd., Zwanenburg Nurseries, Haarlem, Holland. Oncocyclus, regelias, and their hybrids, and bulbous irises are specialties.

Index